Dream Your Dream: Getting Your Writing Out There!

A step-by-step guide to successful writing and publishing

By

Valerie Rose

What people are saying about books by Valerie Rose

You Better Recognize!

"What a great testimony to the power of the human spirit! I recommend this book to anyone interested in personal development. It's a true guide to the pathway of recognizing and utilizing the greatness that lies within us all."

—Desi Williamson, CSP
One of America's top motivational speakers, Author, "Get Off Your Assets!"

"As an author, consultant and motivational speaker, I believe that "You Better Recognize!" is packed with great inspirational messages and can serve as an important "lessons learned toolkit" to take with you along life's journey. Valerie's approach in "*You Better Recognize!*" invites personal growth and discovery."

—Deborah A. Watts,
Author, "101 ways to know you're "black" in corporate America"
President, Watts-Five Productions

"You Better Recognize! A spiritual guide- because life's a "trip" provides readers with ideas on how to build positive self-concepts, self-discipline, self-efficacy, self-initiative, and self-preservation through truisms, heart warming personal stories, poems and quotes. Valerie Rose simply pours her life learning experiences into a soulful literary piece in an attempt to help lift others as she continues to climb toward the light."

—Doctoral Candidate, Ramel L. Smith

"My husband, Jeff, is helping me with the final proofing of the manuscript. He is so into this book that he keeps reading me passages from it. I keep telling him that I've ALREADY READ IT!! He said, 'I know. But, it's the kind of thing you want to share out loud.' "

—Judith Hence, Editor
Henceforth, Inc.

"I was very impressed with the You Better Recognize! It is a wonderful, refreshing read... expect great things..."

–Mechelle Avey, Author, "A Lifetime Loving You"

Cappuccino in the Winter

"A riveting, tender, and emotionally moving story. Valerie Rose has a remarkable talent for creating captivating characters. This beautiful story will live in the heart forever."

—Jacquelin Thomas, author, Hidden Blessings.

"Valerie's excellent choice in words quickly eat up the page, making one avarice to move on to partake of the next delicious course."

—Linda Hudson-Smith, author, Ice Under Fire.

"...The reader enters the cyber world of computers; the plot is littered with intrigue. This novel would set a movie screen ablaze with action, romance and drama."

—Rendezvous Magazine

"*Cappuccino in the Winter* steams with unquenchable passion and subterfuge. Take a sip and I promise you won't be able to put it down until the very last drop."

—Rick Malone, author, Violet of a Deeper Blue

"An exciting tale of corporate politics, romance, and a bit of political intrigue. Here is a book that will call for your undivided attention as the book begins with a bang and only picks up its pace from there! I find myself looking forward to the next story by Valerie Rose!" ***

—Huntress Book Reviews (Reviewed by Détra Fitch)

"...*Cappuccino in the Winter* will delight both computer aficionados and romance fans."

—www.romanceincolor.com

"This is a truly wonderful first novel by a excellent writer...I found it so enticing that I couldn't put it down until it was finished."

—Joyce D. Broderson, MBA, Twin Cities Chapter

The Family Reunion Is Not A Real Vacation

"This playful little book draw smiles from kids and their parents..."

—Mary Ann Grossmann, Book Critic, St. Paul Pioneer and Press

"A WONDERFUL BOOK...INSIGHTFUL...A book for all ages, espousing the virtues and fun of the time honored family reunion."

—Ken Burkeen, Book Channel Manager, BlackVoices.com

"An entertaining way of teaching children to value family."

—F.M. Avey, author The Harlequin's Nutcracker, Girl Gifts

"In just a few short pages, *The Family Reunion Is Not A Real Vacation* took me down memory lane to my own family reunion as a child and as an adult. Valerie Rose connected the dots in showing children how family reunions truly can be a real vacation."

—Sandra King Freeman, Soulful Crosswords

"I think this is a good book for kids to read. It teaches us that it is important and fun to spend time with our family."

—Marlon Watts, Children's Book Reviewer
The Hook Up Network (TheHUNetwork)
Empowerment Zone (e-Zone) Newsletter.

Dream Your Dream: Getting Your Writing Out There!

A step-by-step guide to successful writing and publishing

Summary: A quick reference guide for writers who want to get their work "out there."

Published in the United States by Roses Are READ Productions, St. Paul, Minnesota.

Dream Your Dream is the motivational imprint of Roses Are READ Productions, an organization which produces and publishes books in all genres.

Roses Are READ Productions
C/O Valerie Rose
P. O. Box 7844
St. Paul, MN 55107

To order call: 1-877-430-0044
email: valerie.rose@gte.net

http://www.rosesareread.cc
http://www.valerierose.com

ISBN: 0-9703489-0-8
Library of Congress: 2002093298

Dedication

This book is dedicated
to my mother, father and
two daughters, Samantha and Taylour.

Acknowledgements

Thank you to the Divine Infinite Spirit – for my life.
Thank you Mother and Father – for your love and guidance.
Thank you family and friends – for your encouragement.
Thank you Marie – for your artistic talent and insight.
Thank you Trisha – for your writing tutelage.
Thank you Judith – for your keen editorial eye.
Thank you Milt – for your dedication.
Thank you Avid Press – for opening the door.
Thank you Hillmans – for volunteering your services.

Contents

Dream Your Dream: Getting Your Writing Out There!

A step-by-step guide to successful writing and publishing

Introduction

People always ask me what motivated me to write my book. My answer is that it was not so much a motivation as it was a process. There was no single event that I would call "the" motivation. I didn't just jump up one morning and say, "OK, I think I will write a book today because XYZ happened." It just didn't happen like that. Having a book published was a dream that came to fruition over a period of time, through a series of events.

There has always been something inside of me...a little voice that kept saying, "Hey, you know, you should write a book one day." But I didn't really listen to that little voice until a lot of different things came together that pushed my nebulous dream into my reality.

Ironically, my cloudy muse began to take on some form when I began to experience some rather difficult circumstances in my life. I began to daydream and fantasize about different... better circumstances. Fortunately, I began to write these dreams and fantasies down.

For me, writing was an escape mechanism, sort of a cathartic release. I had no intention of expounding on these ideas until I was talking one day to a woman I work with. Somehow we got on the subject of writing books and she told me that she was talking to an editor at Milkweed Press about having her book published. It occurred to me that this woman, this African-American woman, wasn't just talking about writing a book or dreaming about writing a book, she was actually talking to an editor about having it published. Inside of that moment, the notion of having a novel published became tangible to me.

All of this was brewing in my subconscious one day when I decided to browse the book shelves at a discount store for Sidney Sheldon's latest. Out of the corner of my eye, I noticed a book that appeared to have Black people on the cover. I picked it up and found that it was from a new line called Arabesque from Kensington Publishing, which later became BET books. This again told me that someone was publishing fiction written by African-Americans.

Several days later, I became intrigued with a story about computer hackers that happened to air on a radio news program that I was listening to.

All of these things happened at different times, but they came together to help me push my dream of writing and publishing a novel into my reality.

Today, in addition to being an author, I am a business owner. My company, **Roses Are READ Productions** produced my first novel, *Cappuccino in the Winter,* published by Avid Press. It has subsequently produced and published three additional books, including this one. Its mission is as follows:

> Roses Are READ is a literary production company based in St. Paul, Minnesota. Our mission is multi-dimensional. We wish to promote reading through the production of high quality books of all types. It is also our mission to feature people of color as the primary characters in these books, as it is our goal to give communities of color the opportunity to see themselves in print, as well as to reflect a true and realistic image to the rest of the reading public.

I state all of the above to make a point. My decision to publish a book and start a business was my response to a series of stimuli. In other words, it was a process – a process of life circumstances. So when it comes to getting your writing "out there", you too will make this important discovery. Once the decision to write a book (or anything else) has been made, you will discover, through the process of reading this book, that everything that ensues is also a process. There's a process to writing. There's a process to structuring a story. There's a process to getting your work published by a traditional publishing house. There's a process to self-publishing. And there is a process to promoting, merchandising, and selling your work. Process. Process. Process. There are even processes within processes. So when it comes to getting your writing out there, if that is your goal, you must understand that there are processes that are involved in the successful attainment of that goal.

If you want to get your writing "out there", it is important to understand, be familiar with, and properly implement the steps in each of these processes.

This book is designed to introduce you to and guide you through each of these processes. The goal of *Dream Your Dream: Getting Your Writing Out There!* is just that, to help you get your writing out there. This book is not meant to be a comprehensive instructional manual to getting published, but rather a tool to aid you in the realization of that dream.

My goal and dream was to have my novel, *Cappuccino in the Winter*, published. I, along with a lot of help from people who had faith in me and my work, managed to push that dream into reality. Ever since that time, people have approached me with questions about my personal journey to getting my writing out there.

These and other questions prompted me to write a tip sheet for aspiring writers on how to get published and another one on how to self-promote a book. As I began to be solicited to speak on these topics, I began to see that there was not only great interest in these topics, but also a practical need for a guide that addresses them and related issues, particularly in communities of color. This is because, until recently, people of color were not being published by the major publishing houses unless they already had a name. I saw a need, so I decided to write this book to fulfill that need.

Dream Your Dream: Getting Your Writing Out There! is a quick reference guide that delivers a unique, multi-dimensional approach to helping writers to produce, publish and market a quality piece of work.

The first part of this book, **All About the Process**, is designed as a quick reference guide that addresses the various processes that are involved with getting your writing out there. Each process overview includes a high level outline detailing the procedural steps followed by an explanatory discussion of the key concepts, strategies, and practices involved with each step.

The second part of this book, **Journey to Publication**, is in direct response to the numerous questions that I have received, not only on the writing and publication processes, but also about my own personal journey to publication as well. As a result, this section is simply a compilation of the things I have learned along the way to getting published.
It includes an article detailing my own personal journey, samples, examples, and a frequently asked questions segment entitled, *Just the FAQs Ma'am, Just the FAQs*.

You will see a lot of me in this section. This is because I am opening up my personal files to you, in hopes that it will help you to achieve your dream of being published. What you will see are actual files that were used in my own personal journey. I may have changed a name or two, but most of the documents are actual.

Finally, the third part of this book is a directory of references to books, websites and other resources that could be of interest or help to you as you make your own journey.

It is my hope that ***Dream Your Dream: Getting Your Writing Out There!*** will be useful to you as you pursue your dream of being published.

Section I
All About The Process

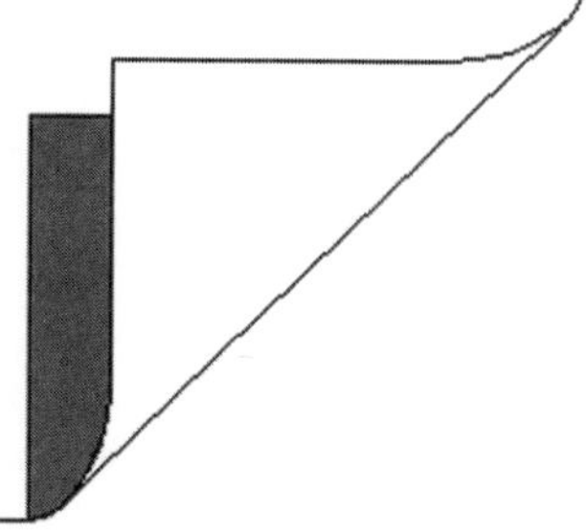

About The Writing Process

Good writing is the successful result of a step-by-step process. When you read a book, story, or article that has a clear, concise, understandable message, it is more than likely that the author took the time to go through at least part, if not all, of the steps in the writing process.

The shortest distance between two points is a straight line. The reality, however, is that very few lines in life are actually straight. If point A is the conception of an idea, and point B is the finished product, the writing process is the line that flows between. That line in between represents a series of steps that are designed to help you implement the organizational structure that you need in order to produce a quality piece of work. Depending on the text that you read, different books use different terminology for the various steps in the writing process, but the methods and practices are basically the same. The steps are intended to give your writing some organization and structure.

Getting from Point A to Point B:

The Steps of the Writing Process

The Writing Process

1. Prewriting
2. Drafting
3. Revising
4. Copy Editing
5. Incorporating Changes
6. Publishing

Step 1: Prewriting

Decide what you want to write.

How do you decide what to write? Maybe you've been given an assignment or maybe you have this concept or idea that you want to develop into a story. Or maybe you just want to write something, but don't know what. The best way to start is to write about something that you know...something familiar. Another choice is to write what you like to read. In other words, if you like romance, write a romance. If you like science fiction, write science fiction.

Determine your purpose.

What is the intent, goal, or objective for the piece that you are writing? Do you want to educate, inform, communicate a message, or just entertain the reader? What do you want people to know or gain from reading your piece? Write your purpose down so that you can refer to or revise it later.

For example: My purpose for writing this book is to introduce you to an overview of the basics in writing and publishing. My intent is to open the door to general guidelines, tips, and references that will help you to get your writing out there.

Think about what you want to say and how you want to say it. If you feel comfortable sharing your ideas, talk with other writers about your ideas. This is called verbal brainstorming.

What is your topic? Do some research. Go to the library. Get on the Web. Find some information on the topic that you are trying to write about. If you are doing a piece set in a special place or time, you have to do some research to be sure that your piece is accurate.

Determine your audience.

Who is your audience? Who is going to read your piece and why? Know and understand your audience. This is so important because different people have different expectations.

When you put your writing out there for others to read, you are putting yourself out there for others to read. And as soon as you do, people are going to start judging it. That's just the way it is. So you have to ask yourself some important questions. How do you want your readers to react? What are your expectations? What are their expectations? How much time do your readers have available to read what you wrote?

This is not to say that you should compromise yourself or your writing. You always want to write what's in your heart. But at the same time, it's important to understand that what's in your heart might get you the results that you want and expect… or it might not. It all depends on the audience.

Who are you trying to reach? What do you want them to gain from reading what you have written? Write from the heart, but understand your audience before you write it.

There are a host of things you must consider when it comes to analyzing an audience, like religious background, cultural background, general age, time availability, educational level, and economic level just to name a few.

If your readers are at the poverty level, do you want them to read about opulence and wealth or do you want to them to read about people who are in similar circumstances? It's up to you. It depends on the message that you want to convey and the reaction that you want to get from your readers.

If you like to write erotica and you are trying to reach an audience that likes to read Christian romances, you might want to reevaluate your priorities or risk alienating the audience that you are trying to reach. If this is not a problem for you, then by all means say what you want to say. Write what you want to write. Just understand the ramifications.

If you know that your audience is primarily Hispanic, then publishing a piece that is readable in both English and Spanish will probably score you some points.

If your audience likes to read romances, chances are they probably won't want to read a story line that focuses on the trials and tribulations of a football player. And the reverse is true as well.

If you plan to write a historical piece set in 18th century England, would your audience have enough education or information to understand what you are talking about? If not, are you going to educate them, simplify your approach and language, target a different audience, or choose a different subject matter all together?

Whatever you are going to write, it's best to know your audience before you write it. Maintaining your integrity and tailoring your message are not mutually exclusive. Generally, you can find a happy medium.

Step 2: Drafting

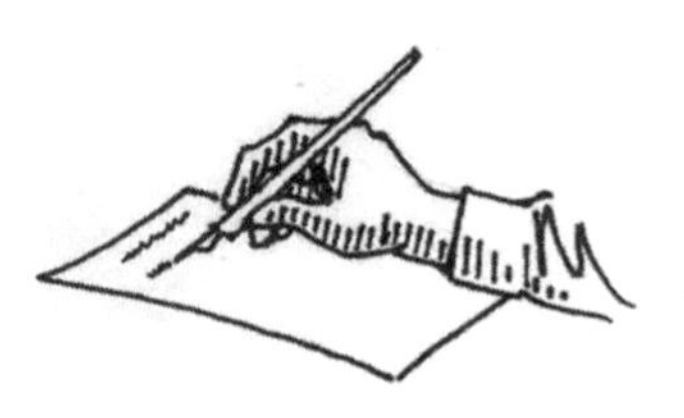

This step is sort of a free-for-all where you try to get all of your ideas on paper or online so that you can have something to work with. This is called free writing or brainstorming on paper.

Sit down with a notebook and a pen and just write whatever comes to mind, even if it's the same thing over and over again. If nothing comes to mind, just keep writing these two sentences over and over again, "I am about to have a marvelous insight. I can feel it." Usually, the repetition brings new insight. Don't worry about the way it looks, you will revise later in the process.

After you've finished your free writing, try to sequence your ideas or pull them together in an outline. Expand the text from each bullet point in your outline and you will have a rough draft to work with. If you are writing a story, there are some important things you need to understand about story structure before beginning your outline. Chapter 2 discusses story structure and details the mechanics of putting a story together.

Step 3: Revising

This step is where you read what you've written and rearrange words or ideas for better readability. Maybe a word doesn't fit; or a paragraph should be added, repositioned, or deleted all together. Maybe you get a new insight and decide to include a whole new section to illustrate your point more fully. Or maybe a character that you've created takes over and starts doing and saying things that take the story into an entirely different direction.

Does your piece say what you want it to say? Does it serve the purpose you stated in step one? If not, then you need to revise it until it does. You may also correct grammar, spelling, style, and consistency in this step. Step 3 goes hand in hand with copy editing, which is the next step.

Step 4: Copy Editing

It's best to have a copy editor review your work. A copy editor can review for a number of different things. You might want him or her to do a second review for readability. The copy editor might change words or phrases, just as you did in the revision step. Or you may ask the copy editor just to proof read, limiting the review to grammar, spelling, punctuation, and consistency. Here the copy editor will make a hard copy of the work and highlight spelling errors, or items that are inconsistent in their appearance. If for example, you used a typeset of Arial 10 point for a heading, but you use `Courier 12 point` for a similar heading later in the piece, a good copy editor should catch this. Be specific on what you want the copy editor to do.

Step 5: Incorporating Changes

In this step, you are simply making the changes in the document that have been identified in steps 3 and then again in step 4. After including the changes, look at the piece in its entirety to make sure that its appearance is consistent with your expectations.

STEP 6: PUBLISHING

In this step, you make the appropriate arrangements for getting the piece to the reader. This could take many forms. The published document could be delivered in any number of different mediums. It could be electronically delivered in the form of an e-mail, website, or pdf (portable document format). Or, it could be an actual printed document. You could print it yourself and deliver it to the reader yourself. Or in a more likely scenario, you would contact a printer or print broker to whom you would hand over the disk or mock-up that contains your piece. The printer will ask you how many copies you want and what kind of paper you want to use for the interior and exterior. The printer will give you a price and deliver the copies to you.

NOTE: If you are going the traditional publishing route, your publisher will take care of Steps 4, 5, and 6 for you.

About Story Structure:

Understanding the process of putting a story together

What is a story?

The *American Heritage Dictionary* defines a story as 1. An account of an event or series of events; narrative. 2. A prose or verse narrative intended to entertain.

"To entertain." Those are the key words. It really doesn't matter what kind of story you are trying to tell or write, the key words are "to entertain" because to entertain (according to the *American Heritage Dictionary*) means to hold the attention of. If you are writing a commercial piece, the ultimate goal is to tell a compelling story. If you are writing a literary piece, the ultimate goal is still to tell a compelling story. Why? Because a compelling story is an entertaining story.

What good is a story if it does not hold the attention of the reader? And how do you hold the attention of your reader? You evoke an emotional response. In other words, make your reader feel something or relate to something, and suddenly you've snagged their attention.

Stories are about life, because life is a story – an emotional story, a personal story. Life is a personal story made up of a series of events that are laced with emotion. Therefore, anyone who can recount the events of their life can tell a story. But to tell a compelling story... that is something altogether different. A compelling story is a story with a good design. And a story with a good design carries a series of events that were well thought out and planned.

But understand that this is not about using formulas. It's about organization and structure. It's about having a framework, a solid foundation from which to work from, so that you can be creatively free to explore character development and other important aspects of your story. That said, it is important to understand that it doesn't matter what kind of story you are trying to tell or write. What's important is to tell a compelling story, because if you've done that, your reader will be entertained and that is the ultimate goal.

What makes a story compelling?

A number of attributes contribute to the production of a compelling story. The primary attribute is interesting characters. Who are they? What do they want? Why can't they get what they want? What obstacles are preventing them from getting what they want? What are they afraid of? What motivates them to go after what they want despite the obstacles:

Revenge? Greed? Jealousy? Love? Desperation? How do they overcome these obstacles? Do they get what they want in the end? Do they get what they deserve? If so, how and at what cost? If not, why? Who are they at the beginning of the story and who are they at the end? In a good story, the characters always change. How did these characters change and why? No one is all good or all bad. What are her good traits? What are his bad traits? What secret are they hiding that invariably gets exposed through the telling of the story? How does it get exposed?

Theme

Another attribute of a good story is usually its theme. A theme is the overall message that you want to convey to the reader. It is the moral of the story, like:

Crime doesn't pay.
Good always triumphs over evil.
Love conquers all.
Life without love is empty and joyless.
Close your heart to love and you close your heart to life.

For example, *Cappuccino in the Winter's* theme is: Love is worth the risk. It's along the same lines as the last two bullet points: *Life without love is empty and joyless* and *Close your heart to love and you close your heart to life*.

What are you are trying to illustrate through the telling of your story? Answer this question and you will have your theme.

Scene and Structure

"Structure is nothing more than a way of looking at your story material so that it's organized in a way that's both logical and dramatic."

–Jack M Bickham
Author, Scene and Structure

When asked to name the components that make up a story, most people will say that a story must have a beginning, a middle, and an end. This is certainly true, but a good story also has organization and structure.

A structure is a pattern, model, plan, or design for your story. It's a method of organizing the parts of your story in such a way that gives it movement and direction. Structure is a guideline that helps you to keep your story on track. In short, structure is the outline or plot for your story.

There are a number of ways to structure a story. I am familiar with four of them:

- ***Aristotle's Incline***
- ***Triple-O (Object, Obstacles, Outcome)***
- ***The Hero's Journey***
- ***The Master Fiction Plot***

Because the method that I am most familiar with is *Aristotle's Incline*, it will be discussed in detail in the next section. You can find out more about *The Hero's Journey* in Christopher Vogler's *The Writer's Journey*, while *The Master Fiction Plot* and *Triple-O* are discussed in detail in Dwight V. Swain's *Techniques of the Selling Writer.*

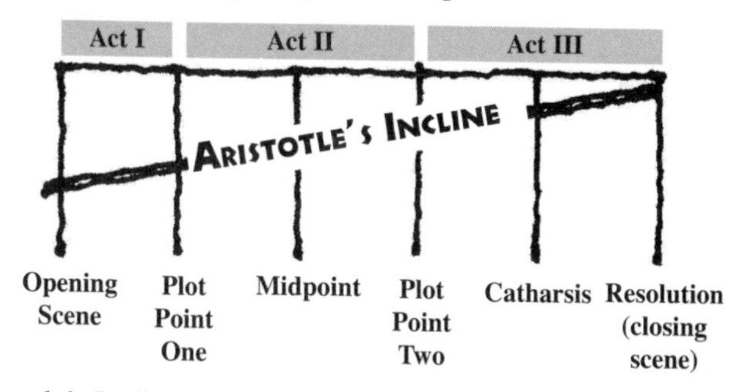

Aristotle's Incline is a visual diagram that illustrates your story line in a diagram. It divides the story into three acts; each act is made up of an alternating series of scenes and sequels.

Within each of these acts are key events that move the story forward, up to a climax, and eventually to an ending.

Scene and sequel are the basic building blocks of fiction. A scene is action oriented...the central character tries unsuccessfully to get what he or she wants. A sequel is when the central character looks back on the previous scene, examines the fallout and decides on a new plan of action to get what she wants.

This alternating scene and sequel construct gives your story momentum. But some scenes are more important than others. These scenes are called "key scenes." And within Aristotle's model, there are six key scenes:

- ***Opening Scene***
- ***Plot Point One***
- ***Mid-Point***
- ***Plot Point Two***
- ***Catharsis***
- ***Closing Scene***

Many novels use this mechanism to establish a plot, so do most screen plays. That said, you can learn alot just from watching movies and looking for these key scenes.

The text below addresses the attributes of each key scene, followed by illustrative examples from movies and the author's debut novel, *Cappuccino in the Winter*. The movies selected for illustration were selected primarily because they happened to have been rented by me or came on television while I was working on the production of this book.

The Opening Scene

This is also known in some models as the *Hook* or *Inciting Incident*. Something dramatic happens right away that kicks the story into gear and gets it moving. Or, the main character's life is suddenly changed.

For example:

Movie/Novel Title	Opening Scene/Inciting Incident
Notting Hill	Travel bookstore owner, William Thatcher (Hugh Grant), physically collides with movie star, Anna Scott (Julia Roberts), soaking her clothing with orange juice.
Shrek	Much to Shrek's dismay, fairy tale characters invade his private swamp.

Movie/Novel Title	Opening Scene/Inciting Incident
Scarface	Tony Montana (Al Pacino) and his friends, after fulfilling an assassination contract, are rewarded with green cards.
Cappuccino in the Winter	After her boss calls her into his office, Alayna Alexander is devastated to learn some unexpected news. Khavon Brighton receives an offer he can't refuse from an unexpected visitor.

Note: It's normal for different characters to have their own story lines, but eventually they should come together.

Plot Point One

This is also known as the *first turning point* in some models. It happens approximately one quarter of the way into a book or about 20 minutes into a movie. This scene is where the character, in response to everything that happened after the opening scene, decides to do something to get his or her life back to normal. The character makes a key decision that propels the story forward, perhaps, even into a different direction.

Movie/Novel Title	Plot Point One
Notting Hill	Anna Scott kisses William Thatcher.
Shrek	Shrek accepts Lord Farquaar's invitation to rescue the princess, in exchange for the deed to the swamp, so that he could get the fairytale characters off his private swamp. In other words, Shrek decides to do something to get his life back to normal.

Movie/Novel Title	Plot Point One
Scarface	Tony Montana travels to South America and meets a drug lord who needs help getting his product into the States. While there, he witnesses the murder of his peer and returns to conflict with his mentoring crime boss. He decides to leave and start his own organization.
Cappuccino in the Winter	Alayna realizes that her attraction to Khavon is problematic. Khavon decides to confront Alayna about their obvious attraction. Alayna tries to get things back on track. She decides to walk away from her feelings for Khavon. Khavon decides to make an unexpected visit to someone in his past. He also discovers that there's more to this computer hacker than meets the eye.

Midpoint

This scene happens about half way through a novel or movie. In this scene something dramatic happens where the character(s) can't turn back. Many times this is where the two main characters make love.

Movie/Novel Title	Midpoint
Notting Hill	Anna Scott and William Thatcher make love.
Shrek	Shrek and the Princess fall in love.

Movie/Novel Title	Midpoint
Scarface	Tony Montana's crime boss, Frank, unsuccessfully tries to have Tony assassinated. In retaliation, Tony kills Frank, takes over the territory, and marries Frank's woman. At this point, Tony has everything that he's ever wanted.
Cappuccino in the Winter	Alayna and Khavon make love.

Plot Point Two

Also known as the third turning point, or the black moment, this scene occurs approximately three-quarters of the way through a story. In this scene, the character experiences a serious set-back. The success and happiness achieved at midpoint is reversed and it appears as if all hope is lost. The character's goal appears to be all but a distant dream.

Movie/Novel Title	Plot Point Two
Notting Hill	Unbeknownst to Anna, William overhears her tell an inquisitive actor that William is a nobody and means nothing to her. William is heart broken.
Shrek	The Princess decides to tell Shrek her secret. Shrek decides to tell the princess that he loves her. But because of a misunderstanding, he decides to turn the princess over to Lord Farquaar to marry. Hurt, the princess leaves with Lord Farquaar with intent to marry him.
Scarface	Tony Montana's wife leaves him. He is the victim of a sting and is in danger of having to serve a prison sentence.

Movie/Novel Title	Plot Point Two
Cappuccino in the Winter	Alayna makes some important discoveries that cause serious setbacks in her relationship with Khavon. Trust is at issue. Khavon is hurt to learn that Alayna doesn't trust him. Khavon begins to question both his instincts about Alayna and his own ability to catch the illusive computer hacker. All of which makes Alayna's dream virtually unattainable.

Catharsis

The rising action in the story builds up to the catharsis. It is the point in the story where everything culminates into an exciting peak. For this reason, the catharsis is also known as the climax. But, the catharsis really consists of two distinct components: The crisis and the climax. The crisis is when the character is brought face to face with his or her greatest fear and is forced to make a decision. The character's choice is usually one that amounts to altruism vs. personal comfort and convenience. The climax is the action fallout that results from the character's decision.

The Crisis Decision

After examining the consequences, the character is faced with a choice. He must choose between:

• something that could get him what he wants and make his life much easier, but would cause deep moral or internal conflict.

• something that would allow him to heal his internal conflict, conquer his fear, or resolve his problem. But this choice is much more difficult, because it can put him in jeopardy or at risk to lose everything—maybe even his life.

Most of the time the character will choose a new course of action that represents the moral high ground, conquering a fear or healing from a

It is in this decision that the character shows what he's truly made of. Who is he really? By giving up his old ideas about life and embracing a new way, or conquering his fear, he demonstrates that he has learned something from the events that took place in the story. He demonstrates that he has changed. Through the process of telling the story, you demonstrate that he has grown.

The Climax

The climax is simply all of the action that happens as the result of the character's decision. What does the character do as a result of the decision? What happens when she does it? How does the world respond to this action? Answer these questions and you will have your climax.

Movie/Novel Title	Catharsis/Climax
Notting Hill	Anna decides to expose her true feelings to William. Afraid that his heart won't recover if he loses her again, William rejects her. William considers the consequences, decides to risk his heart and races after Anna in a fast-paced chase to catch her before she leaves London.
Shrek	Shrek decides that he must stop the marriage of the Princess to Lord Farquaar. He races to the church, interrupts the ceremony, and tells the Princess that he loves her.
Scarface	The South American drug lord offers to make Tony's prison sentence disappear in exchange for his help to plan an assassination. He agrees, but later incurs the wrath of the drug lord because he decided not to follow through with his end of the bargain, as it would require the killing of the *(continued)*

Movie/Novel Title	Catharsis/Climax
Scarface (continued)	target's wife and children too. In a rage, he kills his best friend over a misunderstanding and loses his sister's love and respect. The drug lord vows revenge and sends in his people to kill him.
Cappuccino in the Winter	Faced with the loss of her dream, Alayna decides to follow her heart anyway. Faced with losing their reputation, Alayna and Khavon decide to make a bold move and execute their haphazard plan. Faced with losing the only woman that he has ever truly loved, Khavon makes an important decision.
More Examples	
Austin Powers: The Spy Who Shagged Me	Dr. Evil informs Austin Powers that he has a choice: He can either save the world or save his girl. Austin chooses to save the world, but then goes back in time and saves the girl.
What Lies Beneath	Claire (Michelle Pfeiffer) is faced with the following choices: • Believe her husband's (Harrison Ford's) story that the dead girl killed herself and he just tried to cover it up. Stay quiet about the dead girl; let the issue die and forgive her husband (thereby saving her marriage and returning to the happy

Movie/Novel Title	Catharsis/Climax
	life she'd known with her husband). • Do the morally correct thing and tell her husband that the dead girl's body must be raised. She opts for bullet point two and discovers the truth in a fast-paced climax.

Closing Scene

This scene is known as the *Resolution* or *Wrap Up scene*. What happened to the characters? Does he get the girl? Does she get the boy? Does she save the world? Does he heal his pain? Answer these questions and you will have the closing scene.

Movie/Novel Title	Closing Scene
Notting Hill	Anna and William get married.
Shrek	Shrek and the Princess get married.
Scarface	Tony and his sister are both killed.
Cappuccino in the Winter	You'll have to read the book on this one.

The Final Analysis

Remember that the character should change. How did the character change? Did she go from bad to good? Good to bad? Poor to rich? Was he closed to love and decided to open up?

Your goal is to tell a compelling story. To tell a compelling story you must entertain the reader. How do you entertain the reader? Evoke an emotional response in your readers by making them care about your characters. Your reader gets to know and care about your character by watching them develop and grow through your storyline. This is the reason you need structure.

Final Note: The characters should be more than they appear to be or more than you expect. This is what is meant by the terms, "three dimensional character." Dimension is what makes them interesting. Also, you must understand that happy people are not interesting. If your character is happy, then he or she doesn't need or want anything. How can the character grow or do anything if they already have everything that they want? Your readers don't want to read about a character who wakes up in the morning, kisses her lover, goes off to work and the world is lovely. They want to watch her freak out when all kinds of crazy stuff starts screwing up her life. How does she react? What does she do? How does she handle it? And what is the next crazy thing that happens after she handles the last? How does she handle that one? That's what your readers want to read about.

The best resources I have found on story structure are:

Techniques of the Selling Writer
Dwight V. Swain
ISBN: 0-8061-1191-7

The Weekend Novelist
Robert J. Ray
ISBN: 0-440-50594-1

Story
Robert McKee
0-06-039168-5

Scene & Structure
Jack M. Bickam
ISBN: 0-89879-551-6

The Complete Guide to Writing Fiction
Barnaby Conrad
ISBN: 89879-395-5

Other Resources:

The Writer's Journey
Christopher Vogler

Conflict, Action & Suspense
William Noble
ISBN: 0-89879-634-2

The Writer's Digest Guide to Good Writing
ISBN: 0-89879-807-8

Creating Characters & How to Build Story People
Dwight V. Swain
ISBN: 0-89879-662-8

Building Believable Characters
Marc McCutcheon
ISBN: 0-89879-683-0

How to Write Mysteries
Shannon Ocork

About the Publication Process

About the Traditional Publishing Route

Advantages:

- Production costs. The publishing house covers the pre-production costs; In other words, they put up the investment. There is no cost to you. And you, subsequently, receive royalties from the book.
- Distribution. The publishing house takes care of all the distribution issues.
- Legalities. The publishing house takes care of the copyright and ISBN issues.
- Lucrative deals. There is the potential for a very lucrative deal with a publishing house, but there are many, many factors leading to that end. A lot of things have to be in place for it to happen.
- Constructive criticism. Some rejection letters offer very good constructive criticism that you should listen to.

Disadvantages:

- Validation. You have to wait for someone to validate your work and deem it worthy enough to go into print.
- Rejection letters. Sometimes editors can be very cruel and hurt your feelings.
- Profits. Unless you have a name or have established a record, the amount of money you receive might not meet your expectations. Typically, a publishing house offers "no name" authors a 5 to7 percent royalty rate off either total sales or net sales. Distributors like Ingrams, Baker & Taylor, and Amazon.com take anywhere from 40 to 55 percent off the top. Net sales are the 60 to 45 percent that remains. Total sales do not factor in the distributors discount. For example: If your book costs $10.00 and one book was sold, how much you receive would depend on where it was sold and what is stated in your contract.

Type of sales specified in your contract	Books sales	Distributor's cut at 40%	Your cut is up to 5%, according to your contract.
Total Sales	$10.00	$4.00	$10.00 x 5% = .50
Net Sales	$10.00	$4.00	$ 6.00 x 5% = .30

Either way, this is not a lot of money. Unless you sell a boatload of books, this is not a lot of money.

- Your contract determines your release date. The pressure to meet a date may stifle your creativity.
- Unless you are with a big publishing house and have a fairly good deal, you probably won't have a marketing budget. In short, the publishing house takes the profit while most of the time the marketing and promotion still falls to you.
- Control. You can research and sweat over the details and description of an hierloom sapphire bracelet, but the editor can have the authority to reduce your work to the words 'a piece of jewelry' in the final manuscript. The publisher usually makes all the decisions about the cover, too. That said, some of the smaller publishers, like Avid Press, who published *Cappuccino in the Winter*, encourage and invite direction and input from its authors.
- Time. If you go through the recommended submission process, it can take anywhere from 2 to 5 years to see your book in print. These numbers are not cast in stone, but it can take anywhere from:
  - ✓ 1-2 weeks to receive submission guidelines;
  - ✓ 2-6 weeks to receive a response from a query;
  - ✓ 3-6 months to receive a response from a proposal;
  - ✓ 3-6 months to find out if they want to publish it;
  - ✓ 1-3 years to push it into production.

What do you need to do?

Target a Publisher

After you've decided what you want to write, you need to find out who's publishing it. There are a number of ways to do this. Here are two:

- Find several books in the genre you want to write that have recently been published. Open the inside cover to see who the publisher is.
- Invest in the book: *The Writers Market*. This is available at any bookstore and they publish a new edition every year. This book will give you the names of the editors for the publishers that you have identified in bullet point one. It will also give you the names of editors for the publishing houses that you haven't yet identified.

Write your book.

Using the guidelines in the writing process and story structure, write your book. It is important to do this first because after sending in a query letter, the publisher might ask to see the book. If you don't have one, then what? I recommend completing the manuscript before approaching a publisher.

Request submission guidelines

Every publishing house has specific guidelines that indicate how they want manuscripts submitted. Some want only a query letter. Some ask for a synopsis and the first three chapters. It varies by publisher. So it's important to find out what they want to see and how they want to see it. The way you do this is to write the publisher and ask them to send you their submission guidelines. You will find an example of this in the Samples and Examples Appendix.

VERY IMPORTANT: Enclose a SASE (Self-Addressed Stamped Envelope) with your request. Failure to do this can result in the publisher not sending you the guidelines—or worse, turning off the editor, or both.

Prepare a query letter.

After you get the guidelines, prepare the materials that they want to see.

If the guidelines state that you should send a query letter first (along with a SASE), that's all you send. A query letter is a short letter designed to get the attention of the editor. The objective of a query letter is to catch the eye of the editor so that she will want to see the full manuscript or at least a partial.

Your query letter should be short, to the point, and include a the following:

- An introduction of yourself.
- A brief description of your story.
- Why the editor shouldn't pass on this idea. How your story is different.
- Why will it sell? Does it have a unique subject matter or twist?
- A request to send either the full manuscript or the first three chapters.
- Send an SASE.

Use a general business format for your letter.

Prepare a proposal.

A proposal is a packet that typically contains the following:

- A cover letter. – Remind them who you are, what your story is about, and what's enclosed.
- A synopsis of your book. – This is a 3-5 page summary of your book.
- A bio. – This is one page description of you and your writing experience.
- Sample writings. – Anything that you've written that has been published (optional).
- First three chapters of your manuscript. – See Manuscript Format below.
- Include a SASE.
- Many times it helps to mark your materials on the outside of the envelope as: REQUESTED MATERIAL.
- Even if you get a rejection letter, send them a thank you note for reviewing your materials. It's a refreshing gesture because not everyone does that and editors will remember you for it.

Manuscript Format

The manuscript format that is generally expected and accepted is as follows:

- One inch margins left, right, top and bottom.
- 12 pt. Courier.
- Double spaced.
- 25 lines per page.
- Coversheet with name, address, and word count.

(See figure 2.5 Manuscript and Coversheet in the appendix.)

About Pitching

A pitch is telling an editor or agent about your story idea. Condense your book synopsis into 1 or 2 sentences. For example, my pitch for *Cappuccino in the Winter* is: ***"Cappuccino in the Winter is a story about a computer hacker who hooks up with a former hacker to catch a cyber-thief and the two fall in love in the process."*** Once you come up with your line, you have to practice it over and over again so that it just becomes second nature and you can toss it out easily and effortlessly. I have given my spiel so many times that one time I gave it to someone who asked about the book, and

I left out the part about them falling in love. Then my daughter reminded me, "Mommy, you forgot to say the part about them falling in love."

About the Contract

Don't sign anything until you get an agent or at least have an attorney look at it. (If you don't have the money to hire a lawyer, try calling a law firm and asking if they do pro bono services or contact the SBA and tell them that you are looking for a law firm that does pro bono work.)

Most publishers have a boilerplate contract. A boilerplate contract is a standard contract that is used to begin the negotiation. Contracts vary by publisher. In the Samples and Examples section of the appendix you will find a sample contract from Avid Press.

About the Self-Publishing Route

Advantages:

- Validation. You don't have to wait for someone to validate your work and deem it worthy enough to go into print.
- Control. You are in control. You don't have to worry about researching and sweating over the details and description of a very specific make or brand of car only to find that it may have been generalized to sports car in the final manuscript. You can either fire your editor or simply change it back. Either way, what you see in the final manuscript is what you wanted to see in the final manuscript. No one can tell you what goes in your book. People can make suggestions, but you make the final call. It's all up to you. You are the decision-maker.
- Profits. Profits from direct sales are just that, direct. They go directly into your pocket with no middleman. Once you've demonstrated that there is a demand for your book, you can negotiate a better deal in the sale of your rights, if you do decide to go to a traditional publishing house. This is because the publishing house understands that you can make the money on your own, so they have to offer you something better.
- Time. Depending on what type of book you're writing and if it's already been copy edited, once you hand over your copy, the turnover to see your book in print is anywhere from 4-8 weeks
- You determine your release date.
- You don't have to worry about contract violations.

Disadvantages:

- You cover the pre-production costs; in other words, you put up the investment dollars.
- You take care of all of the distribution issues and distributors always get a cut.
- You take care of the copyright and ISBN issues.
- There is the potential for a very lucrative deal with a publishing house, but there are many, many factors that lead to that end. A lot of things have to be in place for that to happen.

Note: For all hired work, ask for a written estimate and give a limit to the amount that you are willing to spend. This way you won't be surprised with a final invoice that grossly exceeds the original estimate. See The Roses Are READ Connection in the appendix for the names and numbers of all the firms that I hired on for help. Get bids from more than one service provider. Ask for a time frame for completion.

What do you need to do?

Write your book.

Using the guidelines in the writing process and story structure, write your book.

Locate a book designer.

Tell her (or him) that you would like a design for your book cover and possibly the interior of the book. Describe your concept for the cover of your book to your designer or give her free reign and let her creativity take her where it takes her. You might want to give her a copy of the manuscript, or at least a synopsis, so that she understands your idea and can come up with a concept. You want to do this early in the process, so that your designer can have some time to work on it while the manuscript is in the edit or construction phase.

Hire an illustrator.

If you are doing a children's book or you want art on your cover, you will probably want to hire an illustrator. As indicated above, explain your concept and what you want done.

Hire an editor.

Send your manuscript to your editor. Be specific on what you want edited. Grammar? Punctuation? Style? Consistency? Conciseness? Do you want him to incorporate the edits or just identify them so that you can put them in? Does your editor offer a discount if a certain number of errors are still found in the manuscript after you receive it? The editor will make it read more smoothly.

Review the edits.

Review the comments made by the editor. Decide which ones you will keep and bypass. Make the changes to your manuscript.

Send the edited manuscript to the designer.

Generally, you don't have to layout the book in any type of format, your designer will do that for you. The designer will make it look pretty. She (or he) will put it into a software application called Quark Xpress or Pagemaker. Or, if you have the time and the expertise, you can do it yourself. When this process is completed you, your editor, or both should review the manuscript one last time. Afterwards, the manuscript will be placed on CD for the printer.

Printer Liaison.

Once the CD is available, you can use a print liaison or you can go directly to the printer. A printer liaison acts as a go-between, a line of communication between you and the printer. A printer liaison is someone who is very familiar with the printing process. This person will make the general decisions about paper weight and type, etc. You might want to hire one and you might not. You have to look at the advantages and disadvantages and determine what is right for you.

Advantages:

- Time. A print liaison can save you time, he is doing all of the legwork and correspondence with the printer.
- Experience. There's a certain level of comfort that comes from working with someone you trust who has experience in the printing business.

Disadvantages:

- Experience. If the liaison is doing all the legwork and communication, you don't get to experience that part of the process. You don't have the opportunity to learn and gain expertise. You don't have the opportunity to learn the ropes.
- Time. There's another level that you have to go through to get to your final product.

Printer Costs

Printer costs vary and are based on the following factors:

- ***Color or black and white***
- ***Page count***
- ***Size of book***
- ***Paper type***
- ***Number of copies***

Here are some general estimates I have received in the past.

B/W Book Production Costs (1000 copies, 114 pages)	**Dollar Cost**
Editorial Services	$ 700
Book Design	$ 4,000
Print Liaison	$ 300
Copyright	$ 40
ISBN & Bar Code	$ 50
Illustrator	$ 500
Printer	$ 3,251

B/W Book Production Costs (500 copies, 114 pages)	**Dollar Cost**
Editorial Services	$ 700
Book Design	$ 4,000
Print Liaison	$ 300
Copyright	$ 40
ISBN & Bar Code	$ 50
Illustrator	$ 500
Printer	$ 2,763

Color picture book specs: 28 pages, 51/2"x 81/2", 4 color all sides, 10pt. C1S cover, 70# text, saddle-stitched, Quark File provided with all art scanned.

Color Book Production Costs (1000 copies, 28 pages)	**Dollar Cost**
Editorial Services	$ 200
Book Design	$ 4,000
Print Liaison	$ 300
Copyright	$ 40
ISBN & Bar Code	$ 50
Illustrator	$ 1500
Printer	$ 7,200

Color Book Production Costs (500 copies, 28 pages)	Dollar Cost
Editorial Services	$ 200
Book Design	$ 4,000
Print Liaison	$ 300
Copyright	$ 40
ISBN & Bar Code	$ 50
Illustrator	$ 1,500
Printer	$ 3,875

Children's Books

Children's books are generally in full color. As you can see from the cost estimates above for a 28-page book, color is very, very expensive to produce. Learn from my experience: If you elect to self-publish a children's book, you may want to consider doing a hard cover. This is because you are competing with publishers like Disney and Scholastic that can spout out paperback books by the thousands with very low print costs. Therefore, they can price their books at a much lower cost. You, on the other hand, have to price your book a lot higher in order to recoup your investment and make at least a little profit. And believe me, you will hear about this price difference from people. Your readers want to know what's up with that. But with hardcover books, you can compete with the big boys because the production costs are not that different for hard covers. Besides, for kids, a hard cover book is more durable and schools like that.

Should I self-publish?

That question is a bit like asking if you should stay married or get divorced. There's an upside and a downside to both. You have to review the advantages and disadvantages and decide what's best for you.

Section II
The Journey to Publication

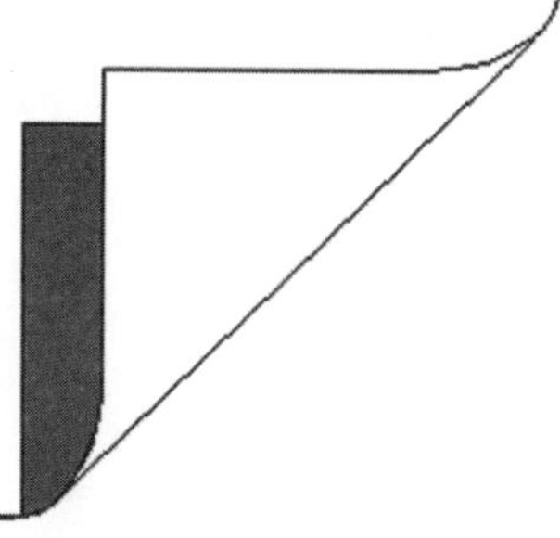

Just the FAQs Ma'am, Just the FAQs.

Frequently Asked Questions

Q. Is *Cappuccino* true?

A. I heard someone say once that any good fiction is "loosely" based on the truth. That said, I will say that there are seeds of truth scattered throughout the story. Each of these seeds grow and blossom into fictional flowers, or "roses" if you will. But I got the computer hacker idea from a story about hackers that aired on the radio. So while there are seeds of truth throughout the story, ultimately it's a work of fiction.

Q. Are the sex scenes true?

A. I generally leave this question up to my reader's imagination.

Q. Where did the title, *Cappuccino in the Winter* come from?

A. It is symbolic. Aside from the fact that I love to drink cappuccino, the protagonists in *Cappuccino* are people of color, and I wanted to give readers some indication of that. The story is set in Minnesota. That's where the winter part came from. It is also meant to symbolize the hot passion of the protagonists in the cold of winter.

Q. How do you find the time to write?

A. I write when I can. I write in long hand over lunch, on the plane, late at night after I put my children to sleep. I write when I'm watching TV, not all the time, but sometimes. Actually, I limit my TV watching, but if I am watching TV, many times I write, too.

Life is about choices: You can choose to be about washing the dishes or you can be about doing something that you enjoy. You can choose to be about doing the laundry or you can choose to be about doing something that brings you satisfaction. You can choose to be about getting a good night sleep, or you can be about doing something to bring your dream into reality. Life is always about choices. I guess what I'm saying is that a sparkling clean house does not necessarily go hand in hand with a successful writing career. It's not impossible to have both, but they don't necessarily go hand in hand.

Q. I want to write a book but I don't know how to get started. How do I get started?

A. Write what you know. Read what you want to write to see how others have done it. Start with an outline. Free write, just to get something on paper to work from. Interview your characters. (See the character interview in the appendix.) Invest in some of the books listed in the resource list.

Q. How much does it cost to self-publish?

A. See the charts in the self-publishing section.

Q. What tools do I need?

A. Any word processing application will work. Most people use Microsoft Word.

Q. How do you overcome writer's block?

A. Try just writing the same line on a piece of paper. For example try this: *I can feel creative inspiration coming forth.* Just write it over and over again, eventually something creative will come to mind. Or, say this prayer before writing: *Thank you, God, forgiving me the creative inspiration that I need to go forward with this piece.* Or, just walk away from it, watch some TV, read, listen to music and come back to it.

Q. Should I use an outline?

A. Using an outline is generally a good idea.

Q. Should I self-publish?

A. Review the advantages and disadvantages and decide what's best for you.

Q. How are you promoting your book?

A. I've been using the things listed in *25 Ways to Promote Your Book* (you can find this list in the appendix.)

Q. Did you design your own website? If so, what tools did you use?

A. Yes. Microsoft Publisher.

Q. Who is your publisher?

A. Avid Press out of Brighton, Michigan (www.avidpress.com) published *Cappuccino in the Winter*. I self-published the rest of my titles.

Q. Do you write in longhand or use a computer? Which is better?

A. I use both. When I am away from my home or don't feel like sitting at the computer, I write in longhand and later transfer to disk. Which is better is a matter of preference.

Q. Where do I end the chapter?

A. Look at the books you want to emulate. Assess the length of their chapters. Where do they end a chaper? End the chapter wherever you want, but always end it at a place that will leave the reader hanging. That way the reader will want to turn the page to find out what happened.

Q. How long did it take you to write your book?

A. I was working a full time job when I wrote *Cappuccino*. It took me three years. It took me about a year to write *You Better Recognize!*

Q. How many books have you sold?

A. I don't talk about numbers. I don't think people understand that when they ask you this question they are really asking you to disclose your personal financial business to them. When someone asks this question, what they are really asking is, "How much money have you made?" Yet, if you were to turn around and ask them the dollar amount of their last pay stub, they would look at you like you were crazy and/or appropriately tell you that it is none of your business. But if you do elect to give an answer, immediately a judgment is made. Either you sold too many books for them, or not enough. That's why I just started to respond with the comment, "I don't talk about numbers."

Q. What kind of a print run did your publisher do for your book.

A. I don't talk about numbers. (For the same reasons stated above.)

Q. How do you obtain a copyright?

A. Mail a request for information on how to obtain copyrights and an ISBN see below:

For ISBN info contact:
R. R. Bowker Company
121 Chanlon Road
New Providence, NJ 07974
1-888-BOWKER2
1-877-310-7333

For copyright info contact:
Copyright Office
Library of Congres
101 Independence Avenue S.E.
Washington, D.C. 20559-6000.
(202) 707-3000(202) 707-9100
http://www.loc.gov/copyright

- or -

The U.S. ISBN agency address is:
U.S. ISBN Agency
630 Central Avenue
New Providence, NJ 07974
Tel: 877-310-7333
Fax: 908-665-2895
isbn-san@bowker.com

For copyright basics go to:
http://www.loc.gov/copyright/circs/circ1.html
http://www.templetons.com/brad/copymyths.html
http://www.bitlaw.com/copyright/obtaining.html#works
http://www.lcweb.loc.gov/copyright/

Character Interview

Use this worksheet to begin your character development. Ask your character the following questions.

What is your name? Do you have a nickname? How did you get it?	
How old are you?	
What color are your eyes?	
What do you like to do?	
When is your birthday?	
What secret are you hiding?	
What are you afraid of?	
What is your marital status?	
Tell me something about your family.	

Why are you unhappy? What would make you happy?	
What kind of car and/or house do you have? What does it look like?	
What vice do you have?	
What strengths do you have?	
What distinguishing mark do you have?	
Where did you go to school?	
What do you want? Why can't you get it?	
What's your favorite color? Food? Drink? Car? Flower?	
How do you normally dress?	

What is your ethnicity?	
Do you exercise? If so, what kind do you do?	
What do you do in your spare time?	
Do you have a job? What is it? Do you like it?	
Where are you from? In what city do you live? Country?	

Resources

How to Get Happily Published
Judith Applebaum
Harper and Row Publishers
ISBN 0-06-010141-5

The Writer's Digest
Guide To Manuscript Formats
Dian Dincin Buchman & Seli Groves
ISBN: 0-89879-293-2

Manuscript Submission
Scott Edelstein
ISBN: 0-89879-398-X

How to Publish, Promote, and Sell Your Own Book
Robert Lawrence Holt
ISBN: 0-312-39619-8

A Complete Guide to Selling Books for the Self-Published Author
Linda Coleman-Willis
ISBN 1890368016

Best Practices

- Adjust the room temperature to make sure you are comfortable.
- If you are writing longhand, get a good pen that flows well, so that you won't be distracted by a pen that you don't really like.
- Find a special place where you like to write. (Remember, you can write longhand and transfer to computer later.) When you find a special place to write, your subconscious knows it's in this place and then creative ideas start flowing.
- Backstory is the character's background. Do not put it all in the front of the book. Slide in bits and pieces throughout the telling of the story.
- Boil your story down to a single sentence. You can use that when people ask what your story is about.
- Interview your characters. See the interview questions in the previous section.

- Write about something you know.
- Send thank you notes to people who help you. Mention them in the acknowledgements of your book.
- Keep a notebook with you.
- During "back to school" sales you can usually find pocket folders for 10 cents a piece. If you are so inclined, you can insert your materials in a folder when making a proposal or media kit submission.
- Reward yourself for making good progress.
- My advice is not to tell your coworkers. It's not that they won't be happy for you; most will. But you don't need them thinking that your writing is more important to you than your job. Even if it is, they don't need to know that. And you don't need them thinking and wondering about that.
- Before you submit your book to mainstream magazines for review, do some research. Especially if you are of color, do some research. Find out where other people who write books like yours are submitting their books to. If your book features a heroine who is ghetto fabulous, you don't want to send your book to a reviewer who is used to reviewing books about heros and heroines who live in 18th Century England. I can't emphasize how important this is. This is because if you get a bad review, at least you know you got a bad review because they didn't like your book, not because they didn't understand the concepts and/or terminology or just couldn't relate to them. If you do some research before hand, at least you don't have to worry that your book got a bad review because it was outside of the mainstream.
- See *Tips for Aspiring Writers* in the appendix.
- Make sure that you spell the editor's and/or agent's name correctly.
- Pray the following prayer before beginning:

I thank you God for giving me the creative ideas and thoughts that I need to go into this writing. Thank you for helping me to move my piece along in an exciting and meaningful way.

Tips for Aspiring Writers

By Valerie Rose

- Read what you want to write.
- Look inside the books you like to read and see who published them. Write the publishing house and ask for their "Guidelines for Submission" or "Submission Guidelines". Guidelines are tips on how to submit your work to the publishing house that you are interested in. Be sure to send a (SASE) Self Addressed Stamped Envelope for their reply.
- Typically, they will ask you for a synopsis of your story or the first three chapters of the book or both. If they like it, they will ask you for the rest of the book.
- Buy some books on manuscript submission, story structure, and character development. And then read them. Some good books to invest in are: *Manuscript Submissions* by Scott Edelstein and Scene & Structure by Jack M. Bickam, *Techniques of the Selling Writer* by Dwight V. Swain, and *The Weekend Novelist*. And of course, *The Writer's Market*.
- Be persistent and determined. Finish the book.
- At least write something down. That way you'll have something to work with.
- When making a submission, always send a SASE (Self Addressed Stamped Envelope) for the publisher's reply.
- Attend a writers conference. But never try to give your manuscript to an editor at the conference unless they ask for it. There are hundreds, sometimes thousands, of writers at these conferences. Even if they wanted to lug it back to whereever there offices are, (and believe me they don't), they would have nowhere to put all the manuscripts that they would receive from all the writers.
- Always label your submission on the envelope, REQUESTED MATERIAL or REQUESTED SUBMISSION.
- Join news groups and mailing lists on the Internet.
- Join "Romance Writers of America" and/or local writing groups.
- Turn off the phone, screen calls when you write. Steal time to write on your lunch break, on the bus, on the plane, on the train...

- Hang out with people who like to do what you like to do. Attend local and national literary events.
- Talk to authors and ask them what they did.
- We are in the information age. A lot of information is exchanged via computers... e-magazines, e-mail, e-publishing. For writers, you have to have a presence on the internet because if you don't, you are operating at a huge disadvantage because there's a wealth of information out there that's just waiting at your fingertips.
- Try not to let the rejections get to you. It's part of the business.
- Listen to the criticism given in your rejection letters, most of the time it is very, very constructive.
- Establish some publication credits to put on your bio. Submit short stories and articles to local/national magazines and newspapers.
- Keep submitting everywhere. Always keep something in the mail.
- Send thank you notes to people.
- Find a special place that you like to write and go there frequently.
- Save all correspondence.
- Believe in your dream, for if you don't who will? Mariah Carey has a song entitled, "Make it Happen!" Listen to this song and let it inspire you.

25 Ways to Promote Your Book

This document was written for the Twin Cities Black Authors group. (This accounts for the local slant on some of the bullet points.)

1. Join an organization like The Midwest Fiction Writers or the Midwest Independent Publishers Association. By virtue of being a member and an author, you can participate in book signing events and for booths, the cost is split among participants. Also, many times these organizations will be contacted for interviews by the media, and by virtue of being a member, you can participate in those, too.
2. Just call up a radio station and say, "Hey... I'm the author of this great new book and I think your listeners would really be interested in it. Would you be interested in interviewing me or doing a promotion?" Do the Freddie Bell Morning Show and Write On! Radio. I have not yet contacted KMOJ, but do their show, too. Contact other media outlets.
3. Join the Loft. www.loft.org . 612-215-2575. Submit some of your material to them for publishing in their magazine: *A View from the Loft*. Write On! Radio is a part of the Loft organization.
4. Make up a press release. Surf the web to see how others have done it and make up your own. People usually have them on their website. For an example, see my website at www.valerierose.com and click press release.
5. Get a website.
6. Make up bookmarks on your pc for a free give away... or have some professionally printed.
7. Hang out with people who like to do the same thing you do... authors, writers, poets, printers, editors...
8. When you go on vacation...Take some of your books... Talk to the hotel manager... and say "Hey... I'd like to set up a book-signing event for the patrons." They will probably do it. This is what I did in Jamaica. A portion of the trip was then tax deductible. And I ended up having a huge photo feature in the Jamaica Tourist Times which I use for promotion.
9. When you go to conferences like the UMBA book festival that are giving away free books, take them and then use them to make up a

promotional give away that will draw people to your table. Go to Walmart or Target and get a clear plastic jar or storage container. On your computer make up a little label that says Register to Win! Cut it out with some fancy edged scissors and paste it on the jar so that people can put their names into it for a drawing. While they are writing their names, you can tell them more about your book so that hopefully, they will buy it... or at the very least, you have their names for a mailing list or a future book promotion.

10. Some of the authors at the First Friday's event had an African throw to put over the table when they were selling their books... I liked that idea.

11. Contact Cushcity.com and other online sellers. Cushcity.com has a catalog that goes out to a large mailing list... you have to pay... but still it's a good outlet.

12. During the Christmas season, I heard an author interview on the radio. I thought, *hey, that's a great outlet*. So I called them up and asked if I could do one. The DJ hesitated and said that they typically only do self help books, but to send him a copy and he would take a look. So I came up with an idea. My book is called *Cappuccino in the Winter*. They give away prizes and stuff all the time. So I went to Starbucks and bought a book of gift certificates for a free cappuccino. Then I wrote the guy and sent him some books with one of the coupons in each book. I wrote a note that said, treat your listeners to a double dose of hot cappuccino! Anyway... nothing happened. I thought they would do something over Christmas... but nothing happened. Then, Valentine's week, the guy calls me up out of the blue and said..."Hey we want to do something..." I was like, "Right now?" He said, "yeah". So I did an on the spot interview... and they were giving away autographed copies of my book for about five days.... Valerie Rose... *Cappuccino in the Winter*.... Valerie Rose... *Cappuccino in the Winter*... Hey it was great.

13. Contact some booksellers in cities that have the demographics that you are trying to market to.

14. Make a copy of your book cover and put it in a picture frame or have a countercard professionally printed to sit on your table.

15. Have articles with good reviews framed for display...

16. Sometimes balloons are nice for a table... Bring your press releases, cards... always carry your cards with you.... you can get free business cards at www.vistaprint.com

17. I highly encourge you to go to writers conferences... to meet people like you...
18. You can have little tiny books made with excerpts from your books either printed professionally or made from your computer.
19. Have candy at your table to attract passers-by.
20. Submit your book to magazines for review and use the reviews on a review sheet to hand out to your readers. **Important:** If you plan to submit your manuscript to a mainstream magazine or e-magazine for review, do some research especially if you are of color or are writing in a specific genre. Find out where other authors who write what you write are submitting their manuscripts to. Try to find out if the magazine has a reviewer that is of color or who frequently reviews culturally sensitive material. At least then if you get a bad review, you know it's because they just did not like the book, not because they did not relate to, like or understand "culturally sensitive" material.
21. Ask other authors for quotes to be placed in or on your book.
22. Read, *How to Publish, Promote and Sell your own Book* by Robert Lawrence Holt.
23. Contact other authors and ask them to give you a quote for your book. It's best to do it before it's printed so the review can appear in or on the book itself. Another big thing that has worked for me is having your reviews printed... Give them a slip of paper that shows other people think your book is great too... I have many, many people come back to me and purchase the book because they read the review sheet that I gave them.
24. Make up a brochure or have one professionaly printed that talks about how important it is to buy books like the ones that you have written... then conveniently include an order form and the ISBN number for your book. And point them also to your website.
25. "Hey you, come over here. I need to tell you about my book!" That works sometimes too! Good Luck!

From Seed to Harvest: A Writer's Journey to Publication

By Valerie Rose

Writing a novel has always been for me sort of a nebulous dream —a literary seedling, if you will. But several events happened to me over time that prompted me to prepare the soil, dig a hole and begin nourishing my freelance notion to see what type of fruit, if any, it would bear.

The right location and environmental conditions are crucial to the success any gardening attempt. I remember being in a bookstore and casually mentioning my dream to the employee who was helping me to find someone else's work.

I told her I was toying with the idea of writing a novel of my own someday. She said something like, "Romantic fiction is really hot. Publishers are always looking for talented authors in the romance genre. It's a good place to start."

I'm not sure if I knew it at that time or not, but I'd found a sunny location with optimal, fertile soil for the planting of my little seedling.

The year's planting and harvest season had come and gone, when the second incident happened... I was chatting with a woman whom I hadn't known for very long when somehow the conversation moved to the subject of writing and getting published. She started telling me how she was talking to this editor at a local press house who liked her work. Suddenly, it occurred to me that the reason why my dream of writing a novel was a nebulous one, was because inside, I'd always thought that writing novels was something that other people do. Now here was this person who, just like me, was an African-American woman who, just like me, was working at an everyday job, even at the same company that I worked for, trying to make a living. Here was this average, everyday, African-American woman, who was just like me, telling me how she was talking to editors and publishers. That was a turning point for me, as suddenly —in one defining moment —I realized that I AM OTHER PEOPLE! And in that moment, I got it. I understood for the first time, I mean really understood, what a significant impact a role model could have on a young African-American life. Because suddenly, you see someone who looks like you, doing things that you thought only other people did. And then you think to yourself, if they are doing that, I can too! And inside of a moment, a dream can go from the intangible to the tangible. And in my case, a nebulous dream can go from cloudy to crystal clear.

And then something else happened...Browsing the paperback section in the store one day, looking for Sidney Sheldon's latest, I was stunned to find what appeared to be an African-American couple embracing on the cover of a book. The pastel coloring of the photograph was a muted blue-gray, so I moved closer, still unsure. *It was arguable,* I thought, *but I think* they're *Black*. I picked the book up and studied it closely. *They are Black*, I thought. *These people on the cover are Black*! I remember standing in the store, dumbfounded, like I had just seen a ghost or something. Eventually, I regained my senses and purchased the book. In case you're curious, the book was FOR ALWAYS by Bette Ford published by then Kensington, Arabesque.

Prior to the 1990's there was a stark mainstream fiction void in the publishing industry. But now with the phenomenal literary and commercial success of Kensington's Arabesque line (now BET Books), Ballantine's One World and Genesis Press, multicultural fiction, with a quiet storm on the marketplace, is finding its voice and other publishing houses are not only taking notice, but following suit.

The climate couldn't be better. The heat from the sunny conditions was warming the soil.

But still I was struggling with what variety to plant, when I heard a story on Minnesota Public Radio about computer hackers. I told my friend that I was going to write something about Black hackers and she commented, "Yeah, they could be computer security experts." *Yes*, I thought, *they could*. I dug a hole for my seedling and turned it over with a spade.

Pestered by the slug of a regular day job, my seed struggled to grow. But I was persistent and determined. The storms of rejection assaulted my delicate, fragile flower. I was devastated, yes, but I chose to use the criticism that I had received as valuable nutrients to make my flower robust, as well as beautiful. I listened to the advice and lectures from editors who'd rejected my manuscript, romance newsgroups and local/national writing groups. I studied books on story structure, pacing and character development. I also started writing and submitting short stories, using what

I had learned, to boost my ego. Two were published in *Jive Magazine*. Another along with one of my poems was published in *Futures Magazine*. I also had some non-fiction work published in a literary magazine called *The View*, produced by The Loft, the nation's largest literary center.

And then one day, out of the blue sky, I got the e-mail! Harvest time! Avid Press chose *Cappuccino in the Winter* to launch their new Kismet imprint. Mmm! Fresh! Delicious!

The moral of the story? A dream, carefully nurtured with patience, persistence, humility, determination and talent, will, under the right conditions, produce fruitful rewards.

To all aspiring authors:

Creativity is the manifestation of the divinity in all of us. The universe is a powerful dynamic, all you have to do is open yourself up to its energy. How? You are the impetus. You are the key. You are a powerful creator... We all are.

Section III
Appendices

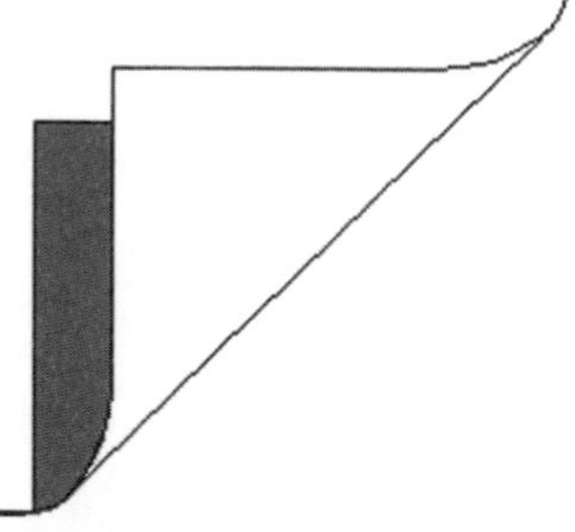

Appendix A

The Roses Are READ Connection

Resources that I have used for the books I've published.

Editor: *Dream Your Dream: Getting Your Writing Out There!*
You Better Recognize!
Henceforth, Inc.
Marketing Communications, Copy editing
E-mail: hence4th@att.net
Website: *www.henceforthinc.com*

Designer: *Dream Your Dream: Getting Your Writing Out There*
You Better Recognize!
(Marie is a wonderful talent and has a heart of gold.)
Associates By Design
3201 N.3rd St.
Minneapolis, MN 55412
E-mail: mlewis@designabd.com
Website: *www.designabd.com*

Cover and Book Illustrations: *Dream Your Dream: Getting Your Writing Out There!*
Avidor Studios
3629 Grand Ave. S.
Minneapolis, MN 55409
E-mail: kavidor@visi.com

Cover and Book Illustrations: *The Family Reunion is Not a Real Vacation*
Simmons Art Studio, Inc.
c/o: Samuel J. Simmons
or Terresa Clark-Simmons
3902 Westbury Drive
Eagan, MN 55123-2087
Phone: (651) 688-2130
Fax: (651) 994-8232

Services:
Illustration of Children's and Adult book themes; General illustrative and Computer output alternatives. Portrait painting by commission, Children and Editorial Cartooning.

Graphic/Layout Artist: ***The Roses Are READ Productions logo design***
Adrian Crawford
acrawford420@msn.com
(651) 222-1244

Creative Graphics by Dana
Freelance Graphic Designer
drudnik@qwest.net
(651) 452-8810
(651) 253-1201

Promotion: All of my publications
Deborah A. Watts
Watts-Five Productions/Publishing
"A marketing and management consulting group"
1161 Wayzata Blvd, East Suite 42
Wayzata, MN 55391
(763) 476-8677 office
(888) 472-2422 Toll free
(952) 891-6545 "New Book Hotline"

Services:
Marketing Stategies/Publishing consulting, publicist, author/book/event promotions, media/public relations and bookings for public speaking and author appearances.

Deborah Watts is a published author, workshop presenter on workplace issues, frequent radio and TV guest, motivational speaker, and marketing consultant.

Associate Publisher: *Dream Your Dream: Getting Your Writing Out There!, The Family Reunion is Not a Real Vacation, You Better Recognize!*

Beaver's Pond Press, Inc.
Coaching and Mentoring Writers to Become Self-Published Authors

Beaver's Pond Press, Inc. is a unique, one-of-a-kind book publishing house. Providing a full menu of traditional publishing and marketing services, Beaver's Pond Press has served over 265 self-publishing, award winning authors nation-wide in the past three years. Beaver's Pond Press has grown from a part-time effort of 25 books per year to 111 book-related projects in 2001. Our 2002 projected goal is three new titles per week.

Milton E. Adams
Direct & Voice Mail: (952) 829-8818

Email: Self-publishing@BeaversPondPress.com
Website: *www.BeaversPondPress.com*

5125 Danen's Drive, Edina Minnesota 55439-1465

Publisher: ***Various writings***
(Barbara Lakey published some of my early work. She also published my daughter's short story, entitled *The Glass Bottom Boat*.)
Barbara J. Lakey
Publisher/Futures Mysterious Anthology Magazine
3039 38th Avenue South Minneapolis, MN. 55406
(612) 724-4023 babs@suspenseunlimited.net
www.futuresforstorylovers.com

Futures Mysterious Anthology Magazine is now in our 5th year of publishing. Each quarterly is packed with approximately 120 pages of short stories and much more.

What could be better? Multi-genre fiction from professional authors like Henry Slesar whose teleplays on Alfred Hitchcock Presents thrilled then and thrill today, to the best new, some never published writers of today. *Starting Line* features new first time ever stars! BRIDGES brings you Ashok Banker from India, and Scott Masterton from Blaine, MN, with viewpoints on the same topic each issue. For humor, mystery, horror, romance, science fiction, literary works....stories from 200 words to novella length....FMAM has it all. Visit our online store at *http://www.futuresforstorylovers.com*. Back issues as well as current and preorders all available. For information contact publisher, Babs Lakey at babs@suspenseunlimited.net; submissions via email only, guidelines are on our website or in every issue.

Photographer: *The Family Reunion is Not a Real Vacation*
(Portland did most of the book design for the *Family Reunion* book.)
Portland Jones
Graphics Design
(405) 692-5330

My name is Portland Jones and the company is Graphic Perfection. I am a graphic designer and have been a photographer for over eleven years. I also freelance for *The Black Chronicle News Paper* in Oklahoma City and I have been doing that for six years. Services: Book cover designs and typesetting.

Address: 922 S. W. 97th Oklahoma City, Ok 73139
(405) 691-1845 office/fax

Photographer: *You Better Recognize!* And *Dream Your Dream: Getting Your Writing Out There.*
(Joshua did the photo on the back covers of *You Better Recognize!* and *Dream Your Dream: Getting Your Writing Out There!*)
Joshua Ivory
Digicomp Image
3335 Morgan Ave North
Minneapolis, MN 55412
(612) 522-3327

Appendix B

Books to Check Out

Techniques of the Selling Writer
Dwight V. Swain
ISBN: 0-8061-1191-7

The Weekend Novelist
Robert J. Ray
ISBN: 0-440-50594-1

Story
Robert McKee
ISBN: 0-06-039168-5

Scene & Structure
Jack M. Bickam
ISBN: 0-89879-551-6

The Writer's Journey
Christopher Vogler

The Complete Guide to Writing Fiction
Barnaby Conrad
ISBN: 89879-395-5

The Complete Idiots Guide to Getting Published
Sheree Bykofsky and
Jennifer Basye Sander
ISBN: 89879-395-5

Conflict, Action & Suspense
William Noble
ISBN: 0-89879-634-2

The Writer's Digest Guide to Good Writing
ISBN: 0-89879-807-8

Creating Characters & How to Build Story People
Dwight V. Swain
ISBN: 0-89879-662-8

Building Believable Characters
Marc McCutcheon
ISBN: 0-89879-683-0

How to Write Mysteries
Shannon Ocork

A Complete Guide to Selling Books for the Self-Published Author
Linda Coleman-Willis
ISBN 1890368016

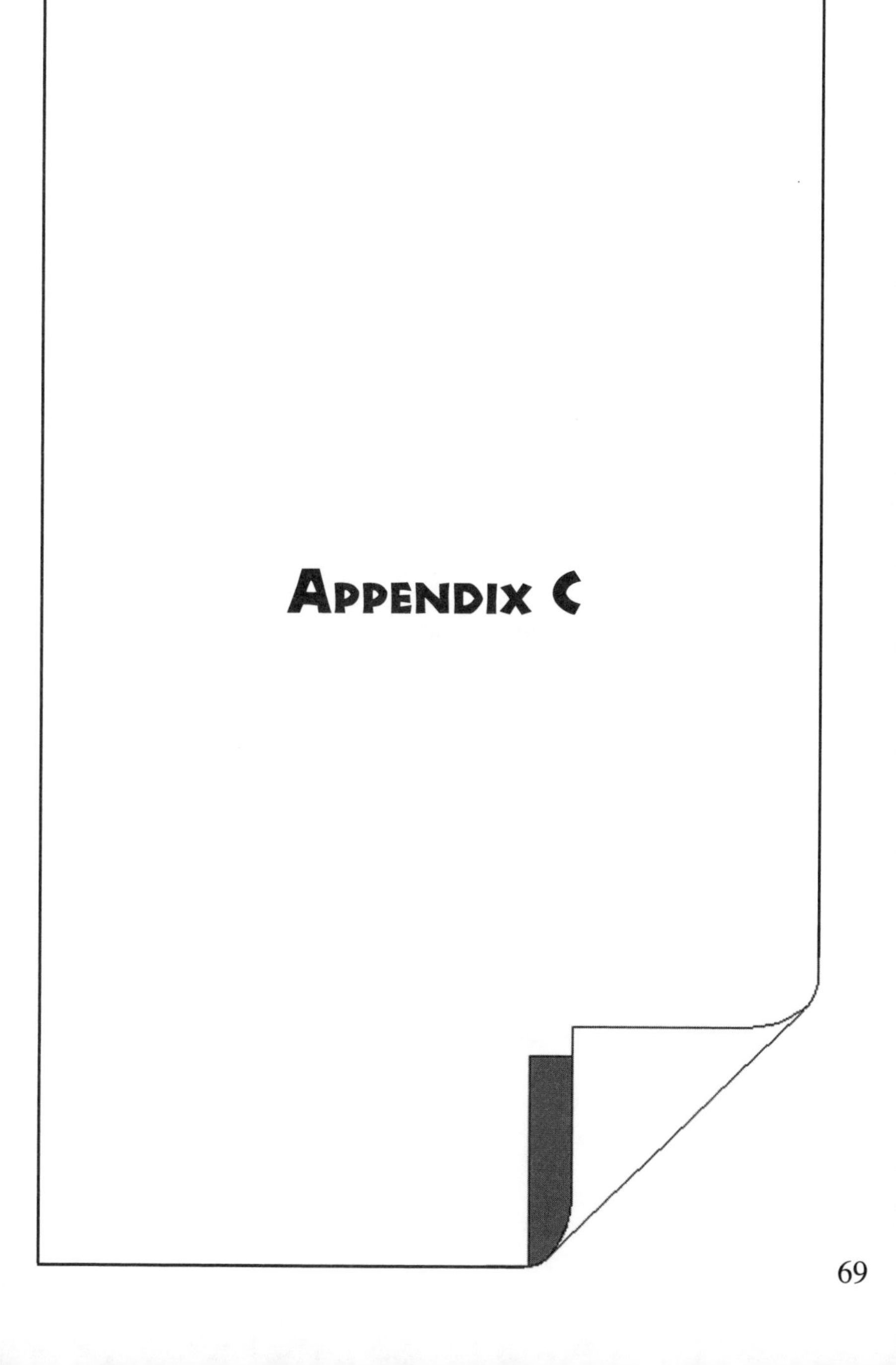

Appendix C

Websites to Check Out

Best Search Engines

Site Description	*URL Address*
Google	*http://www.google.com/*
Alta Vista	*http://www.altavista.com/*
Amazon.com	*http://www.amazon.com*
Deja News	*http://atgratis.com/key/dejanews.htm*
Yahoo	*http://www.yahoo.com/*

Online Booksellers and Promotional Markets

Site Description	*URL Address*
Cush City.com	*http://www.cushcity.com/*
All Black Books	*http://www.allblackbooks.com*
Amazon.com	*http://www.amazon.com*
Powell's	*http://www.powells.com/ebook/ ebookeditions.html*
Barnes and Noble	*http://www.barnesandnoble.com/*
Black Issues Book Review	*http://www.AALBC.com/WRITERS/black.html*
Irmine's Book Store	*http://www.irmines.com/*

References

Site Description	*URL Address*
Black Caucus of the American Library Association	*http://www.bcala.org/*
The Romance Slam Jam	*http://www.romanceslamjam.com/*
Black Voices.com	*http://new.blackvoices.com/* *http://www.blackvoices.com/*

Print Magazines

Site Description	*URL Address*
Futures Magazine	*http://www.firetowrite.com/* *http://www.affairedecoeur.com/* *http://www.firetowrite.com/*
Affaire Decoeur	*http://www.affairedecoeur.com/*
Black Voices.com	*http://new.blackvoices.com/* *http://www.blackvoices.com/*

Writers Resource Websites

Site Description	*URL Address*
Focus: Fiction	*http://www.sat.lib.tx.us/Fiction/fictionindex.htm*
Genre Resources Mystery, Romance, Sci-Fi & Fantasy, Westerns, Horror and Historical	*http://www.sat.lib.tx.us/Fiction/* *fictionindex.htm#Genre*
Fiction Resources Author Info, Books in Series, Publishers and Book Stores	*http://www.sat.lib.tx.us/Fiction/* *fictionindex.htm#More*
Black Erotica	*http://www.erotica-readers.com/* *ERA/GuidelineFrames.htm*
Poetry Magazine	*http://www.poetrymagazine.com/poetry.htm*
Electronically Published Internet Connection	*http://www.epicauthors.org/*
General Writing	*http://www.eclectics.com/epic/*
Netlingo	*http://www.netlingo.com/pocket.html*
The Writing School	*http://www.writingschool.com*
Suite 101	*http://suite101.com/* *http://suite101.com/WritingCenter/*
Black Voices.com	*http://new.blackvoices.com/* *http://www.blackvoices.com/*

A World of Writing ....*http://www.writing-world.com/*
Tips for writers
around the world

Crossing the threshold........*http://www.wire.net.au/~melinda/publishd.htm*
Screen Writers....................*http://www.screenwriters.com*
http://hollywoodnet.com/Johnson/wdetect.htm

About Self-Publishing

Site Description ***URL Address***

Pneuma Design...................*http://www.pneumadesign.com/books/info.htm*

Beaver's Pond Press...........*http://www.beaverspondpress.com/*

Xlibris.................................*http://www2.xlibris.com/*

Associates By Design.........*http://www.designabd.com/*

Books Just Books..............*www.booksjustbooks.com (excellent resource)*

Xlibris.................................*http://www2.xlibris.com/*

Iuniverse.............................*www.iuniverse.com*

10 Big Myths......................*http://www.templetons.com/brad/*
About Copyrights *copymyths.html*
Explained

Obtaining............................*http://www.bitlaw.com/copyright/*
copyright protection *obtaining.html#works*

Grants, Foundations and Monies

Site Description ***URL Address***

$25,000 Loft Award in.......*http://www.loft.org/conmckni.htm*
Children's Literature
(1 grant)

ABC New Talent................*http://www.abcnewtalent.disney.com/*
Development
Fellowship
Disney

A mentorship program.......*http://www.loft.org/coninrds.htm*
for Asian American *http://www.loft.org/about.htm*
& Pacific Islander
writers

The Jerome Foundation.....*http://www.jeromefdn.org/*

The loft contests ....*http://www.loft.org/contests.htm*
and grants

The loft mentor series –
poetry and fiction
competition........................*http://www.loft.org/conment.htm*

The Grant Makers..............*http://www.fdncenter.org/funders/*
Finding Funders

Top 100 Ranking –............*http://fdncenter.org/grantmaker/*
Giving Foundations *trends/top100giving.html*

The foundation center –.....*http://fdncenter.org/*
your gateway
to foundations

The Loft –..........................*http://www.loft.org/*
(for spoken word)

SBC ....*http://www.sbc.com/About/*
Foundation/grant.html

Nicholl Fellowship ....*http://www.oscars.org/nicholl/index.html*

Sundance Institute.............*http://sundance.org*

Austin Film Festival..........*http://www.austinfilmfestival.com*

National Endowment.........*http://arts.endow.gov*
for the Arts

Another list of ....*http://www.mcf.org/mcf*
grant makers *whatsnew/gr_list.htm*

Go to www.google.com and enter the key words: "donor forum" for more grant resources.

Online Magazines

Site Description	*URL Address*
Shades of You	*http://www.sormag.com/*

General Information

Site Description	*URL Address*
Dictionary	*http://www.dictionary.com/*
Thesaurus	*http://www.thesaurus.com/*
Authorlink, Unique on-line information service for editors, literary agents, writers and readers.	*http://www.authorlink.com/aserv.html* *http://www.writelinks.com/*
Inks spot	*http://www.inkspot.com/*
The Writer's Handbook	*http://www.geocities.com/Athens/Delphi/4003/writer.html*
US Copyright Home Page	*http://lcweb.loc.gov/copyright/* or *http://www.loc.gov/copyright*
The Loft Literary Center Writer's Resources	*http://www.loft.org/resourcewr.htm*
Prolific Writers Network	*http://www.prolificwriters.org/*
Writers' Federation of Nova Scotia Romance Writing	*http://www.chebucto.ns.ca/Culture/WFNS/romance.html*
Romance Writers of America	*http://www.rwanational.com/*
Book Publishers Links Page	*http://www.ranas-world.com/pub.html*
A Complete Guide to Selling Books for the Self-Published Author	*http://www.lindaspeak.com/selling.htm*

Other Sites of Interest

Site Description	*URL Address*
Minnesota Artists Online	
General Writers Resources	*http://graphicdesign.miningco.com/library/weekly/aa112098.htm*
	http://www.romanceslamjam.com/
	http://www.midwestfiction.com/
	http://www.midwestfiction.com/Main_stuff/joinmfw.htm
	http://www.rwanational.org/
	http://www.writerspace.com/chat/bookaholic-chat.html
NETLINGO	*http://www.netlingo.com/pocket.html*
Books Just Books	*http://www.booksjustbooks.com*
Black Radio Guide	*http://www.radioblack.com*
Focus: Fiction	*http://www.sanantonio.gov/library/fiction/index.asp?res=800&ver=true*
Internet Language Dictionary	*http://www.netlingo.com/pocket.html*
Online Writing Lab (OWL) on Quoting, Paraphrasing, and Summarizing	*http://owl.english.purdue.edu/handouts/print/research/r_quotprsum.html*
The Art of the Article	*http://www.1099.com/c/co/gw/lf/linda018.html*
Query Letters	*http://www.1099.com/c/co/gw/lf/linda017.html*
Self Promotion	*http://www.1099.com/c/co/gw/lf/linda030.html*
United States Copyright Office	*http://lcweb.loc.gov/copyright/*
Alphasmart	*http://www.alphasmart.com*
About National Meetings	*http://www2.h-net.msu.edu/%7Eswpca/meeting.html*
Black Issues Book	*http://www.aalbc.com/writers/black.htm*
Writers Resources	*http://www.loft.org/resourcewr.htm*
Tips for writers	*http://www.tipsforwriters.com/*

Writer's Store.....................*http://writersstore.com*

Visual s of Publishing.........*http://clix.to/visualsofpublishing*
Online

Fiction...............................*http://www.fictionworks.com*

Character Development.....*http://www.esva.net/~davidpoyer/cdf1.htm*
in Fiction

The Writer's Handbook.....*http://www.geocities.com/Athens/Delphi/4003/writer.html*

Authorlink.........................*http://www.authorlink.com/aserv.html*

Crossing the Threshold.....*http://www.wire.net.au/~melinda/publishd.htm*

Prolific Writer's Network *http://www.prolificwriters.org/*

Write Links........................*http://www.writelinks.com/*

All About Romance..........*http://www.likesbooks.com/home.html*

Black Writers.....................*http://www.blackwriters.org*
BWRC

Writers' Federation...........*http://www.chebucto.ns.ca/Culture/WFNS/index.html*
of Nova Scotia

PW Daily...........................*http://www.publishersweekly.com*
for Booksellers
from Publishers Weekly

Writers Guild of................*http://www.wga.org/*
America-West

UCLA film program.........*http://www.filmprograms.ucla.edu/*

E-books

Site Description	***URL Address***
More Resources................	*http://www.avidpress.com*
	http://ebooks.searchking.com/
	http://www.knowbetter.com
	http://www.tomjoyner.com
	http://www.blackvoices.com
	http://www.blackenterprise.com
	http://www.everythingblack.com

Beaver's Pond Press..........*http://www.beaverspondpress.com*
Hardshell..........................*http://www.hardshell.com*
Diskuspublishing..............*http://www.diskuspublishing.com*
Avid Press..........................*http://www.avidpress.com*

Black Literary

Site Description	*URL Address*
Black Literary	*http://www.mosaicbooks.com* *http://www.blackwriters.org* *http://www.prolificwriters.org* *http://www.allblackbooks.com* *http:// www.bitbooks.com*
African American Literature Book Club	*http://www.aalbc.com/*
Black Literature Café	*http://clubs.yahoo.com/clubs/blackliteraturecafe*
Black Images	*http://www.blackimages.com/*

Business and Financials

Site Description	*URL Address*
Financial	*http://www.datachimp.com/articles/financials/fundamentals.htm* *http://www.valueline.com/vlu/4-index.html*
How to Build a Business Plan	*http://www.sba.gov/starting/indexbusplans.html* *http://www.bplans.com/* *http://www.bizmove.com/small-business/business-plan.htm*
Free Business Cards	*http://www.vistaprint.com/*

Appendix D

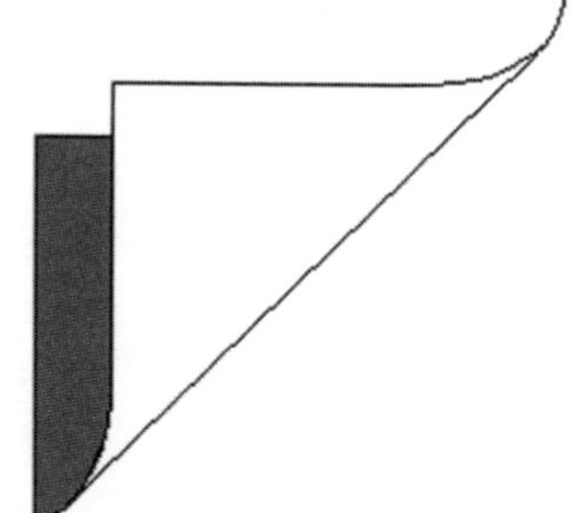

Glossary

Blurb — *A quick one or two liner that summarizes your book.*

Consignment — *Payment for books only when sold.*

Catharsis — *The peak point in the story where the character must make a decision (crisis) and deal with the consequences of her decision (climax). It occurs right before the closing scene.*

Contract — *A signed, binding agreement between you and a publisher or agent.*

Closing Scene — *The last scene in a story, where everything is resolved and the story comes to an end.*

Copyright — *A formal registration of your creative work that legally declares you as the owner of all rights to that work.*

Excerpt — *A short sample of your story.*

Genre — *A category of literature, like romance or science fiction.*

Guidelines — *A list of attributes that should be followed when submitting a piece to a publishing house or grant foundation.*

Hook — *The first event in a story where something happens to get the story rolling. It happens right away in the story.*

ISBN — *Stands for International Standard Book Number. Typically found on the back cover of books, it is a 10-digit number that gives unique identification to books and related products.*

Inciting Incident — *The first event in a story where something happens to get the story rolling. It happens right away in the story.*

Media Kit — *A folder of information about you and your books that is given to the press or publishers.*

Midpoint — *The third key scene in a story structure where the characters are at a point of no return.*

Option — *A clause in a contract that basically indicates how many books the author must allow the contractual publisher to view before the author can show it to someone else.*

Opening Scene — *A key scene that contains the first event in a story where something happens to get the story rolling. It happens right away in the story.*

Pacing — *The momentum/alternating speed and unfolding of a story.*

Partial — *A proposal that contains an excerpt of your book, typically 3 chapters.*

Pitch — *A persuasive conversation given to an editor, a agent or publisher designed to sell them on your book idea.*

Plot point one — *A key scene where the character must make a decision or something happens that moves the story along to the midpoint. It takes place approximately 1/4 of the way into a story.*

Plot point two — *A key scene where the character seems to have no hope of getting what she wants. This is also known as the black moment. It takes place approximately 3/4 of the way into a story.*

Plot points	*Key scenes in a story where something dramatic happens.*
Promo Flyer	*An advertisement for an event or a book.*
Proposal	*A packet of information designed to convince an editor or publisher to publish your book. It usually contains an excerpt from your book and information about you, the author.*
Rejection letter	*A letter that comes from an editor or publisher that informs you that they do not wish to publish your book at this time.*
Royalty Percentage	*A percent of the sales from a book that belong to the author.*
SASE	*Self-Addressed Stamped Envelope.*
Sell sheet	*A promotional flyer designed to sell your book.*
Story Structure	*A framework of events from which to build your story on. A method of organizing the parts of your story.*
Sub-Genre	*A category literature that falls under another category. For example: Romance is genre and Inspirational is sub-genre of romance.*
Synopsis	*Typically, a 3-5 page summary of your story.*

Appendix E

Energy for your-Self

Ingredients:

2 tablespoons lemon juice (1/2 a lemon or use Minute Maid Frozen Lemon Juice in the black and yellow box)
1/2 cup of distilled water (it can be warm)
2 tablespoons of PURE maple syrup (not imitation)
A pinch of red, cayenne pepper

The above recipe was given to me for energy and circulation. But, I tend to use a lot more lemon juice, maple syrup, and red pepper. I usually put it in the microwave oven and drink it like tea.

Appendix F

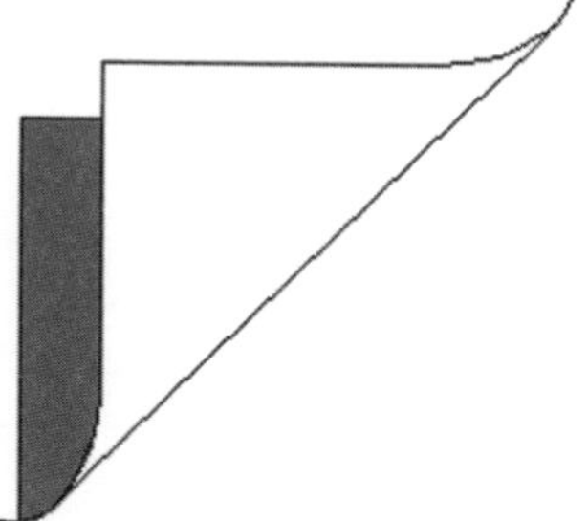

Samples And Examples

Table of Figures:

SAMPLE (Fig. 1.1)

(Request for submission guidelines from a publishing house)

Valerie Rose
900 Queens Blvd.
Crystal, Minnesota 55100
(612) 896-9292 (W)
(612) 298-5292 (H)
(612) 938-2922 (Fax)
e-mail : *valerie.rose@gte.net*

August 20, 1998

Ms. Rebecca Gillian
Managing Editor
Heartsong Presents
P.O. Box 719
1810 Barbour Drive
Uhrichsville, OH 44683

Dear Rebecca:
Please send me the guidelines for Heartsong Presents.
Thank you,

Valerie Rose

SAMPLE (Fig. 1.2)

(Request for submission guidelines from a grant foundation)

Roses Are READ Productions
P. O. Box 7844
St. Paul, MN 55107
(612) 383-2828 daytime;
(612) 394-3728 evening;
Fax: (612) 472-2982

E-mail: *valerie.rose@gte.net*
Website: *www.valerierose.com*

September 24, 2001

Intermedia Arts
McKnight Interdisciplinary Fellowship Program
2822 Lyndale Avenue South
Minneapolis, MN 55408

Please send me the guidelines and/or requirements for the year 2000 Intermedia Arts McKnight Interdisciplinary Fellowship Program and the McKnight National Interdisciplinary Fellowship Residency in Minnesota.

I have enclosed a SASE for your convenience.

Thank you,

Valerie Rose

SAMPLE (FIG. 1.3)

(Response to invitation to submit)

Valerie Rose
900 Queens Blvd.
Crystal, Minnesota 55100
(612) 896-9292 (W)
(612) 463-2728 (H)
(612) 938-2922 (Fax)
e-mail: valerie.rose@gte.net

August 31, 1998,

Ms. Kim Terry
Editor
Kensington Publishing Corp.
850 Third Avenue
New York, NY 10022

Dear Ms. Terry,

I have received your response letter regarding the partial submission for my manuscript, Cappuccino in the Winter. Per your request, I have enclosed a copy of the entire manuscript for your perusal.

Additionally, your response letter cautioned against allowing the mystery element to take over the story. As a result, I did a summary review of the action in each chapter of the manuscript. I looked for places where the mystery element might be construed as taking over the story. While I did make a few changes to the story, by and large, the story as a whole, focuses primarily on the romance and intense sexual tension between the two protagonists. In writing the piece, I tried to follow the guidelines set by some of the other Arabesque books already in print. However, if in reading the manuscript, you think the story is a good story, but you have problems with the mystery element, or you have other issues with the book, please keep in mind that I am very open to editorial input, revision, and/or instruction.

Finally, I have enclosed a post card on which I would appreciate your noting that you have received this material, as well as a stamped, self addressed envelope in which the editorial reply checklist can be returned to me. If my proposal does not interest you, simply let me know via the editorial reply checklist. There is no need to return the manuscript, please recycle as I have additional copies.

I look forward to hearing from you.

Sincerely,

Valerie Rose

Encls.

SAMPLE (Fig. 2.0)

(Query Letter)

Valerie Rose
P. O. Box 7844
St. Paul, MN 55107
(612) 494-4948 daytime;
(612) 393-3987 evening;
Fax: (612) 473-1822
E-mail: valerie.rose@gte.net
Website: www.valerierose.com

January 6, 2002

Mr. Edward Collins
Dream Your Dream Filmworks
192 Tulip Street
Los Angeles, CA 91210

'Code Red': The virus that will not die

Dear Mr. Collins,

This was the headline on August 10th in the Tech section of the USA today (online version). Underneath the headlines, were 19 bullet points of related links. In the last few weeks, there has been a proliferation of stories in the news media about a computer virus dubbed "Code Red" and another called "The Worm", that infiltrates and infects computer networks. And who is it that is wreaking havoc on all these poor unsuspecting Fortune 500 and dot-com companies?

Well, the stereotype is a White male teenager, who finds a judgement free friend in a wired box. And why White? Because most people have trouble believing that a Black man could be smart enough to be a computer hacker. But if there was a Black hacker, surely he could not be the best. Well in my book, Cappuccino in the Winter, the hero is the best and he knows it. Khavon Brighton is a former computer hacker turned computer security specialist who teams up with computer virus expert, Alayna Alexander on a top-level computer security project. In an exciting plot that stretches across the Atlantic to Amsterdam, Holland, the two work to catch the cyber-thief that is wreaking havoc on their system and their reputations.

I know this book would make a wonderful movie. Especially in today's climate, with the explosion of the internet, the e-business boom, and hackers having a field day with it all. Computer security is not only a challenge for the government and the general public, but as evidenced by today's headlines, it's an important strategic initiative for businesses, as well. I would love to see this book optioned into a movie.

My name is Valerie Rose. I live in Minneapolis, Minnesota and I am the author of several books. If you are even remotely interested in doing a film adaptation on a book that has a unique perspective on the subject of computer hacking, please allow me to send my novel to you. I hope that you will give the project every consideration. If you require additional information, I invite you to visit my websites at www.valerierose.com , www.rosesareread.cc or to contact me directly with the contact information in the letterhead.

I look forward to hearing from you.

Sincerely,

Valerie Rose

SAMPLE (FIG. 2.1)

(Requested Query Letter)

Valerie Rose
P. O. Box 7844
St. Paul, MN 55107
Phone: (612) 943-4763

January 6, 2002

Ms. Lori Tenninson
Dream Your Dream Publishing
192 Tulip Street
Los Angeles, CA 91210

Dear Ms. Tenninson,

It was a pleasure meeting you at the RWA National Conference last week. Thank you for taking the time to chat with us in the group interview and especially for taking time out to meet with me individually. I knew that your time was limited, so I really appreciated that.

Per your request, I am planning to submit a copy of my writing samples, and a resubmission of a partial for my manuscript, Cappuccino in the Winter, as there have been several revisions to it since it was first sent to you. You may recall that it is a 100,000 word contemporary romance set in Minneapolis, Minnesota. Although the cast is diverse, the primary characters are African American.

Please expect my submission in a day or two. Once again, it was a pleasure, and I look forward to your request to see the entire manuscript, which is complete.

Sincerely,

Valerie Rose

SAMPLE (Fig. 2.2)

(Proposal Cover Letter)

Valerie Rose
P. O. Box 7844
St. Paul, MN 55107
(612) 555-4350 daytime;
(612) 538-5665 evening;

August 6, 1998,

Ms. Linda Ficocelli
Editor
Harper Paperbacks
10 East 53rd Street
New York, NY 10022

Dear Ms. Ficocelli,

Per your request, enclosed is a partial for my novel, Cappuccino in the Winter.

Falling in love with a handsome young prince and galloping away with him into a hazy, peach orange sunset, is a romantic concept that most young girls in America, irrespective of race or background, embrace and ultimately grow up to anticipate. But what happens when a young, intelligent, African-American woman approaching her thirtieth birthday, living in a state where African-Americans make up less than three percent of the population, has yet to experience what had been implicitly promised to her as a child? What happens to her psyche when she realizes that the deafening sound of her biological time clock is tied to the dismal reality that is African-American women out number African-American men four to one in the place that she has called home for more than seven years? My book, Cappuccino in the Winter, brings this unique perspective to the traditional romance model as it explores these questions and others.

The African-American experience in America is a multifaceted one, rich with intrigue, complications and unique cultural dilemmas. But sadly, particularlyro-

in the romance genre, we have rarely seen it in print until here of late. The African-American love story, as evidenced by the growing numbers of readers, is a fascinating one for the reader to explore. My book uncovers a fictional account of one such experience.

Based in Minneapolis, Minnesota, Cappuccino in the Winter is an 100,000 word contemporary romance which tells the story of Alayna Alexander, a thirty year old African-American computer virus specialist and what she is willing to sacrifice in order to have the promised utopian dream.

While the story revolves around a plot of computer espionage, vandalism, and wire fraud, the core of the story explores the complicated relationship between Alayna, and a former computer hacker turned security specialist, Khavon Brighton, whom Alayna finds herself in love with. Conflicting the story is Alayna's engagement to Warren Harrington, an ambitious and pretentious finance executive whom she does not love, but who offers the prospect of a beautiful brown babies and a warm place to call home. Further complicating the story is Khavon's tortured past which has caused him to vow never to marry again.

The computer bandit hunt takes Alayna and Khavon across the icy Atlantic to Amsterdam, Holland, where they are swept into an underground community of computer hackers, saboteurs, virus writers, anarchs, and computer vandals. Adding flavor and texture to the story, is the close but complicated and mutually envious relationship between Alayna and her best friend, Sheila, who is married with two children.

Cappuccino in the Winter is cast against a pearly, white backdrop of frosty evergreens, ice laden branches, and crystalline snow flakes. It is the steamy romance of two people who fall in love, despite their seemingly divergent goals. Alayna and Khavon's winter love affair is one that will warm the reader's heart. But at the same time, the intimate story is one that is certain to intrigue and educate as it dispels the myth that African-Americans do not use or understand high technology.

If the story idea has sparked your interest at all, you may be somewhat curious about the author. I graduated from the University of Wisconsin - Milwaukee, with a degree in computer science in 1986. A mother of two young children. I have worked for St. Paul based 3M Corporation as a systems design analyst for more than eleven years. I am an active member of the Romance Writer's of America and as you know, attended the national conference this summer. I am a regular subscriber to the romance writers' list digest on the internet and have been an avid reader of African American romance since it became available. I have traveled abroad and been published in the Black Data Processing Journal, Minneapolis Spokesman, and St. Paul Recorder. I have also been published twice in Jive Magazine, a national

African American Romance magazine. The first story, Saying Goodbye, is in the October issue and is probably just hitting the stores. The second story was written on the request of the editor based on a story idea that she had. That story, Jilted Love, is currently in press, scheduled for release in the November issue. These articles and short stories can and will be made available to you upon your request.

Please be advised that this is a multiple submission.

If you are interested in seeing the book described above, I can send you the complete manuscript on disk or paper, which ever you prefer.

Enclosed please find a synopsis and the first three chapters of the book, per your indications at the conference. Also enclosed is an editorial reply checklist for your convenience. Additionally, I have enclosed a post card on which I would appreciate your noting that you have received this material, as well as a stamped, self addressed envelope in which this material can be returned to me, if necessary.

I look forward to hearing from you.

Sincerely,

Valerie Rose

Encls.

SAMPLE (FIG. 2.3)

(Long Synopsis)

Cappuccino in the Winter

A Synopsis

Set in the snowy twin cities of Minneapolis/St. Paul, Cappuccino in the Winter features as the heroine, Alayna Alexander, an attractive, thirty year old computer virus specialist. It tells the story of Alayna, and what she is willing to risk in order to attain a 'colorized' version of the 'Cinderella' dream. A dream that had been implicitly promised to her in the countless books and movies that she consumed as a child growing up in the foster care homes and institutions of Chicago.

Given up as a baby after her father was killed in Vietnam, Alayna grew up longing for the family she never really had. Still clinging to the increasingly dim hope that a benevolent family would someday adopt her into their own, and having languished in the system for more than sixteen years, Alayna learns of the financial incentives in place to keep children like her trapped in in-state care. Disillusioned and demoralized, Alayna becomes determined to establish a family of her own.

After graduating from University of California-Berkley on academic scholarship, Alayna is aggressively sought after by Excelsior Securities, a computer security firm based in Minneapolis, Minnesota. After making the populous Scandinavian metro her home for more than seven years, Alayna, an African-American woman, at the persistent and deafening behest of her clanging biological time clock, suddenly comes to a despairing realization. Although relatively happy in her job and in line for yet another promotion, she suddenly realizes that living in a state where Blacks make up all of three percent of the population, she may never marry, and at best her prospects are severely limited.

But then, Alayna's best friend, Sheila, fortunate enough to have beaten the odds herself, introduces Alayna to her husband's fraternity brother, Warren Harrington. Warren, a pretentious finance executive, whose career is certain to stagnate unless he has a socialite wife at his side, proposes to her. Alayna weighs her options, and untrue to her heart, accepts his proposal. Finally, despite the fact that she feels no love for Warren, Alayna is happy or so she thinks.

As the story unfolds, confusion in the form of a tall, dark stranger slips into her life like an uninvited guest, to upset her meticulously and neatly arranged plans.

When the US Department of the Treasury, as a result of the 1997 congressional mandate, announces it's intention to convert the government's cumbersome, error ridden, tax collection system from paper to electronics, Minneapolis based Liberty National Bank is hand picked by Commissioner Theodore Mulcahy to be the designated financial agent for the project. But when Liberty, experiences a series a wire transfer heists on the back-up security system that was designed by Excelsior several years earlier, Liberty gets nervous. After some convincing, however, the bank agrees to let Excelsior keep the contract to develop the security system for the new tax system, but only on one condition. They must hire a reputable outside security consultant to be the technical lead on the project.

Enter the tall, dark and dangerous hero, former computer hacker turned security specialist, Khavon Brighton. Khavon had a stellar reputation and a solid w column when it came to designing and installing computer security systems. As a child growing up on the North side of Minneapolis, Khavon's parents had given him a Commodore 64 computer for Christmas. They had hoped that it would pull him out of a self imposed, despondent withdrawal resulting from the death of his younger brother from a fire that he was responsible for starting. It worked. Notorious on-line under such pseudonyms as The Eclipse, David Shadowhawk, and Captain Midnight, Khavon gains the coveted respect of his cyber peers as one of the best hackers in cyberspace. But Khavon is stunned when he secretly monitors an electronic conversation between two hackers who change their tune after they learn that he is Black. Hurt and betrayed, the context of that fifteen year old conversation haunts him everyday and pushes him into a constant and unquenchable need to substantiate his skills by squashing those that choose to challenge them. But when Khavon takes on the challenge at Excelsior, for the first time in his career, he is baffled by the cyber thief's constant ability to penetrate his security safeguards. But unbeknownst to Khavon, the illusive hacker is being aided with information from his embittered x-wife, Cassandra who is incarcerated for manslaughter. The pain of his former wife's betrayal continues relentlessly to haunt Khavon, forcing him to remain steadfast in his personal vow never to marry again. The thick, sexual tension between Khavon and Alayna eventually leads to a confrontation, in which Alayna admits to the attraction, but explains that she is still unwilling to sacrifice everything just for what amounts to a few nights of carnal pleasure.

Not long after, Alayna learns that Warren has accepted a position in D.C. without discussing it with her. The altercation leads to their eventual separation.

Meanwhile, Khavon and Alayna continue to clash out of frustration, until Alayna finds herself stranded in a Minnesota blizzard. The two consummate their burning love over a romantic snowy weekend at Khavon's suburban home and eventually become a couple. The dazzling romance of the Christmas holidays with Khavon far surpasses Alayna's dreams. But the fantasy is short lived when Alayna begins to suspect that her heart is the key pawn in a dangerous game of corporate espionage. But love prevails, as Alayna decides to trust the man who will help her track the digital footprints of the computer vandal who is now trying to frame her.

Ultimately, Alayna's limited view of the world is broadened as the computer bandit pursuit takes she and Khavon across the icy snow capped waves of the Atlantic to the city of diamonds, Amsterdam, Holland. It is here that the thief converts the transferred funds into diamonds, for irreversible gain.

After a brief sight seeing tour of the city, the climax of the story takes place at Amsterdam's Schiphol Airport. Alayna and Khavon come up with a hasty plan to retrieve the diamonds from the cyber thief, who turns out to be Mark Olsen, one of their co-workers. The plan of distraction works. In a diversion orchestrated by

Khavon, Alayna manages to strip the diamonds from Mark and looses herself in the airport crowd. But before she can get out of the airport, she literally runs into Warren, her x-fiancé. Warren, Alayna learns with a gun shoved into her side, had been working together with Mark all along. A standoff ensues between Warren, Khavon and undercover FBI agent, Frank Ryan, alias Ted Mulcahy. Alayna is critically injured with a gunshot wound as Warren unsuccessfully tries to escape. Devastated and frightened at the near fatal loss of his only true love, Khavon marries Alayna and gives her the family she has always wanted.

SAMPLE (FIG. 2.4)

CAPPUCCINO IN THE WINTER

By Valerie Rose

Here's a brief synopsis

Discouraged by the statistics of living in a state where African-Americans make up a mere three percent of the population, computer security expert Alayna Alexander decides to marry a man she doesn't love in order to ensure her dream of having a family. But confusion in the form of tall, dark Khavon Brighton, a former hacker, slips into her life when she is assigned to work with him on a top-level computer security project. Sparks fly as the two race to thwart a desperate cyberthief who has a personal vendetta against Khavon.

Here's a one line blurb:

Cappuccino in the Winter is about a computer virus expert who hooks up with a former hacker to catch a cybertheif and the two end up falling in love in the process.

Here's another one line blurb:

You Better Recognize! is an inspirational guide to recognizing the light, the joy and the power within.

.

SAMPLE (Fig. 2.5)

(Manuscript with Cover Sheet)

Valerie Rose
2919 Lockheed Road
Golden Valley, MN 55938
(651) 463-32 Daytime;
(651) 493-5299 Evening
email; valerie.rose@gte.net
website: http://www.valerierose.com

Approximately 100,000 words

Cappuccino in the Winter

A Novel by

Valerie Rose

Acknowledgments

First and foremost, I give praise, glory and thanks to the divine infinite spirit, the Lord, my God, who relentlessly continues to guide, strengthen and sustain me through this wild, perplexing ride we call life.

To Oscar, who was my Black knight--the promised prince, incarnate, who scooped me up and whisked me away to destinations that I had only dared to tour in the recesses of my mind. For that, the good times, the passion of yesteryear, and our beautiful daughters I will always be eternally grateful.

To Mommy's chocolate jewels, Samantha Elayne and Taylour Alexandria for your extraordinary personalities and the sheer joy that you bring to my life.

To my mother and father who gave me unconditional love, time and time again. Thank you for being wonderful, loving parents and giving me the kind of childhood that as a child I assumed everyone had, but learned as an adult that I had been truly blessed.

To my sisters and brothers, Stella, Helen, Elzie Jr. and Jerome for your loving support.

Thank you also Colleen Gleason Schulte and Kate Gleason for your insightful editing skills and for respecting my voice. But most of all for believing in this story and the message behind it.

Thank you to all of my family and friends who encouraged me pursue my life's dream.

Thank you to Soul Sistas, my online internet support group: Michelle J., Alicia, Jackie T. and Jackie H., Cecilia, Karen, Michelle M., and Carmellia. Special thanks to Michelle J. and Alicia for keeping it real--you know?

Thanks to my friend, Renee, who when I told her of my intent to write a story about Black hackers, said something like... "yeah, they could be security experts." Thanks also for introducing me to the internet. Thanks also to Paula for schooling me in html and web page construction.

I would like also to extend a special thanks to literary artists, Sandra Kitt, Eboni Snoe, Jacquelin Thomas, and Linda Hudson-Smith, all of whom have set in my mind, shining examples of kindness for me to follow.

I have never met Neale Donald Walsch, but I would like to thank him for bringing to me the voice of the creator, in the form of *Conversations with God*.

ONE

"Wait a minute, what do you mean you're bringing in someone else?" Alayna said, uncrossing her legs, her mink brown eyes wide with disbelief and betrayal.

Suddenly, the room was a cyclone and she was at the center of it. She'd been certain that Furi had called her in to tell her that the post vacated by Lars when he took the early retirement package was now hers. Finally, she'd thought, finally she was going to get the promotion that for her, was long overdue. Now apparently she'd thought wrong.

Michael Tafuri ran his hand through his thick, gray streaked hair. His olive skin was ashen as he relayed the news.

"Bring in someone else or lose the account. That's what we were told." Furi's hooded lids fell hard and fast. "It's out of my hands, Alayna. Liberty's stockholders aren't happy. When they got wind of this last incident, they gave us an ultimatum."

"But I don't understand. Why? I found the hole and plugged it! I don't believe this. You're bringing someone else in? To do what? What are you saying, Furi? Am I being fired or what?"

Alayna moved instinctively to the window, her vision blurred with a hot salty rush. The unwelcome snow on the other side of the glass was fast and furious. It would be dark soon——ordinarily, a sure indication of that winter would be coming soon. But not today. Today it was already here.

"No. Of course not. Nobody's getting fired. It's just that well——"

Why Furi was hedging? Alayna wondered. They've always had a good working relationship. He'd always been straight with her.

"Well, what?"

"Well, it's your qualifications," Furi spat quickly in one breath, as if that would take the sting out of it.

Alayna gasped audibly. "My qualifications? What about my qualifications? I helped bring Anti-Viral to record profits five years out of seven. What do you want?"

"That's just it. Your background is in virus fighting. They want to bring in someone with a background in electronic fund transfer technologies."

"I studied EFT at Berkeley. You know that as well as I do."

"They want someone with practical experience."

"How am I supposed to get practical experience ifæ"

"We just thought——"

"We? I thought it was they," Alayna raised her voice, not bothering to mask her irritation.

"It is they, Alayna. But frankly, my neck is on the line with one. You know as well as I do that this isn't the first security compromise that we've had in recent months."

"I know, but——"

"Now that Liberty is the designated financial agent for USE-TAX, they're getting a lot of heat from Washington. The Federal Reserve doesn't want to take any chances."

Defiantly, she pushed back the brimming hot tears and turned to face him. Arms crossed, she leaned on one leg.

"So let me get this straight. I've been working on this project for almost six months and you're just going to hand it over to some bureaucrat who knows nothing about the business practices of either Excelsior or Liberty, or the government for that matter, to create a secured environment for USE-TAX?" Alayna was incredulous.

"No. We're just bringing someone in who has some experience in EFT fraud to balance the process. Besides he's not a bureaucrat. He's a well-respected computer security expert. I mean this guy's credentials are impeccable. Besides we need some objectivity. He'll be able to catch things that we might miss. And..."

"And what?"

"And I didn't have a choice. Washington was very specific when they said bring in someone else."

Alayna eyed Furi carefully. "Who is it? Am I going to be reporting to this person?"

"No. Absolutely, not. You both report to me. Equal responsibility and equal authority. It's just that we can't afford another screw up."

"It wasn't a screw up, it was just a little glitch. You can't expect to get everything the first time out, Furi. You know that as well as I."

Furi nodded. "I know, but since Liberty has agreed to keep us as their security sub-contractor, we have an obligation to make sure this thing flies. We're all working toward the same goal here."

Yeah, we're all one big happy family. I am not believing this. "Who is it?" she asked, again.

"Khavon Brighton of Brighton Securities——out of Minneapolis."

The name sounded familiar. She'd heard of the firm. Alayna turned back to the window. She wanted to scream. She'd thrown herself into her work to try to forget. To try to forget what had happened. Just exactly how much drama am I supposed to tolerate in one year -- one lifetime for that matter, she wondered, glowering down at the black, slushy streets below. The only thing she hated more than winter in Minnesota was winter in Minnesota in September. Ridiculous. Whoever heard of a snow storm in September? Only in Minnesota. She didn't even have time to whine and complain that it would be coming soon. How depressing. But no matter. At least this winter would be the last one that she'd have to endure. Warren hated winter as much as she did. After the wedding she'd planned to talk to him about moving south anyway. She'd heard Atlanta was nice. Atlanta, Charlotte...someplace...anyplace but here. Living here was a only constant reminder of what happened. Besides, it wouldn't take her long to revise her resume.

Furi ran his hand through the curly waves in his thick mane.

"Listen, you know that if there was anything that I could do, I would. But the whole thing is out of my hands."

"I know," she nodded. Whatever. I'm out.

"I know this past year has been rough on you, with everything that's happenedæ"

Alayna shook her head and motioned for him to stop. "Does the team know?"

"No. Not yet. I plan to make the announcement at the team meeting."

"So when does this new expert start anyway?"

"Monday."

Alayna turned back to him. "You guys don't waste any time do you?"

SAMPLE (Fig. 2.6)

(Thank You Note)

Valerie Rose
P. O. Box 7844
St. Paul, MN 55107
Phone: (612) 943-4763

January 6, 2002

Ms. Lori Tenninson
Dream Your Dream Publishing
192 Tulip Street
Los Angeles, CA 91210

Dear Ms. Tenninson,

It was a pleasure meeting you at the RWA National Conference last week. Thank you for taking the time to chat with us in the group interview and especially for taking time out to meet with me individually. I knew that your time was limited, so I really appreciated that.

Per your request, I am planning to submit a copy of my writing samples, and a resubmission of a partial for my manuscript, Cappuccino in the Winter, as there have been several revisions to it since it was first sent to you. You may recall that it is a 100,000 word contemporary romance set in Minneapolis, Minnesota. Although the cast is diverse, the primary characters are African American.

Please expect my submission in a day or two. Once again, it was a pleasure, and I look forward to your request to see the entire manuscript, which is complete.

Sincerely,

Valerie Rose

SAMPLE (FIG. 3.2)

About the Author
Valerie Rose

Valerie Rose is a business owner, motivational speaker, and author of several books. Her debut novel, Cappuccino in the Winter - a romantic suspense is set in the Twin Cities, was chosen by Michigan new comer, Avid Press, to launch their new Kismet imprint. A recommended new title in Black Issues Book Review, Cappuccino, although released in December 1999, is still doing well, selling out at both the 2001 and 2002 Romance Slam Jams. Her second release, a children's book entitled, The Family Reunion is Not A Real Vacation, is also doing well.

A guest author at the 2001 Congressional Black Caucus Foundation, Valerie is also the owner of Roses Are READ Productions, which has produced a range of literary art including her newest nonfiction release, You Better Recognize! When asked about her new book, Valerie says, "It's a spiritual guide because life's a trip!" Her fourth book, Dream Your Dream: Getting Your Writing Out There! is scheduled for release in April 2002.

Valerie's writing credits have appeared in many local and national venues, including The View (from the Loft), Futures Magazine, Jive Magazine, The Black Data Processing Journal, The St. Paul Recorder and The Minneapolis Spokesman. And her many appearances run the gamut, including among others: Milwaukee Public Television's Black Nouveau (news magazine program), Write On! Radio, The Freddie Bell Morning Show, nationally syndicated ABC Radio Network, Twin Cities Women of Color Expo: The Gathering, The Jamaican Observer Tourist Times, and Shades of Romance, an online magazine.

As part of the University of Wisconsin-Whitewater's African American Heritage Lecture Series, she was one in the list of distinguished speakers that included, Wisconsin Senator: Gary George, Jazz Musician: Manty Ellis, and Milwaukee Journal/Sentinel Columnist: Eugene Kane.

Valerie is a member of the Loft Literary Center, The Romance Writers of America and the Midwest Fiction Writers. She lives in Minneapolis with her two children, where she is busy at work on her next project. To learn more about Valerie, see her web page at www.valerierose.com. **Visit also:** *www.rosesareread.cc* **and** *www.thetriangleheads.com.*

SAMPLE (FIG. 3.3)

(Short Bio)

Real short bio:

Valerie Rose is the author of CAPPUCCINO IN THE WINTER, a multicultural novel set in the Twin Cities of Minneapolis/St. Paul. Her short stories, poems and non-fiction articles have been published in the Minneapolis Spokesman, St. Paul Recorder, The Black Data Processing Journal, The View, Futures and Jive Magazines. Valerie lives in Minneapolis, Minnesota. Website: http://www.valerierose.com

SAMPLE (Fig. 5.1)

(This is a copy of an Avid Press Publisher Contract and provided as an example of what some publishers offer for standard contracts).

Avid Press, LLC

Publishing Contract

This Contract is entered into as of _______________ (date) by and between

Avid Press, LLC, a limited liability corporation organized and existing under the laws of the State of Michigan, located at 5470 Red Fox Drive, Brighton, Michigan, 48114 (hereafter known as "Publisher")

and

___________________ **(Author)**, a resident ________________________________
_________________________ (Address) (hereafter known as "Author")
concerning a work presently known as ________________ ***(Title)*** (hereafter referred to as "The Work").

This Contract is entered into in good faith, and signatures from all parties named herein indicate acceptance and agreement to the terms described herewith. This Contract shall be considered legal and binding in all countries. Should any legal dispute arise, the laws of the State of Michigan shall be applied and any legal action involving such disputes shall take place in the State of Michigan.

I. Grant of Rights

A. The Author, on behalf of herself and her heirs, executors, administrators, successors and assignees, grants the following exclusive worldwide rights to the Publisher:
   i. to produce, publish, and sell in electronic format (including electronic download, disk, CD, or any other digital format known or to be invented) the Work in all languages, including English;
   ii. any additional rights granted by the optional Print Format Addendum executed by Author and Publisher as stipulated in the Print Rights Addendum.

B. All rights to the Work not specifically granted to Publisher in this Contract and any Addendum are hereby retained by Author.

II. Royalties

A. Publisher agrees to pay Author a royalty of **30%** in US$ of the retail download price (of US$), for each electronic copy of the Work sold, regardless of format or version.

B. Royalties shall be calculated and paid no later than the 30th of the month following the end of each calendar quarter for sales during that quarter.

C. No royalty shall be paid on paper or digital copies distributed for review, advertising, publicity, promotional purpose, sample, or other similar purposes; or on copies sold below or at cost, provided free to the Author, or sold to the Author at a discount of 40% or greater.

D. Publisher will issue to Author an annual 1099 Miscellaneous Income Form in accordance with US Internal Revenue Service guidelines to reflect any compensation paid during the year.

E. Publisher agrees to pay Author **50%** of any royalties or other payments gained through any sublicense agreements. These additional royalties shall be paid in the first royalty check due Author after payment of said royalties is received by Publisher

III. Author's Warrantees

A. Author hereby represents and warrants to the Publisher the following:

i. that he/she is the sole author of the Work;
ii. that the Work is original and that no part of the Work was taken from or based on any other literary, dramatic, or musical material, or from any film or graphic arts, except as identified in writing by Author;
iii. that the Work does not infringe upon any copyright or proprietary right, common law or statutory law; and does not contain any material of a libelous or obscene nature, or violation of privacy rights;
iv. that the Work is not in the public domain, and that the Work has not been published in any format with any company that may still own proprietary rights to the Work;
v. that the Author holds the full power and authority to grant these rights;
vi. that these representations contained herein are true on the date of the signing of this Contract.

B. Author agrees to hold Publisher harmless and indemnify Publisher and its subsidiaries or affiliates, against any claim, demand, action, suit, proceeding, or any expense whatsoever arising from claims or infringement of copyright or proprietary right, or claims of libel, obscenity, invasion of privacy, or any other unlawfulness based upon or arising out of the publication or any matter pertaining to the Work.

C. Author also warrants that he/she will not hereafter enter into any agreement or understanding with any person or entity which might conflict with the rights granted Publisher herein during the term of this contract.

IV. Manuscript

A. On or before ___________ **(date)**, Author agrees to deliver to Publisher copies of the completed Work as follows:

i. one printed, double-spaced complete copies of Work, and
ii. one version on computer diskette in an acceptable format as described on "Manuscript Format Sheet."

B. Author shall also, at the time of submission of final Work, include written authorizations or permissions for the use of any copyrighted or other proprietary material which appears in the Work, including but not limited to art, illustrations, or quotes. These permissions and authorizations shall be obtained at Author's own expense.

C. Publisher reserves rights of final approval on final Work submissions. Author shall be notified of

D. Author is responsible for maintaining backup copies of Work; Publisher is not liable for lost or defective diskettes.

E. Publisher reserves the right to reject the Work and terminate this Contract if Author fails to meet above-mentioned deadline, or if Work is not acceptable for any other reason.

F. Publisher retains the right to edit and revise the Work for any and all uses described under this Contract, provided that the meaning of the Work is not materially altered without the Author's knowledge. Publisher shall have the right to produce, advertise, promote, and publish the Work in a style in which Publisher deems appropriate to the Work, including format, pricing, and distribution.

V. Copyright & ISBN Numbers

A. Publisher shall register the Work in the Author's name in the U.S., and, if necessary, in appropriate foreign nations, under the Universal Copyright Convention and the Berne Convention, showing Author as the owner and holder of copyright to this Work.

B. Publisher has obtained the following International Standard Book Numbers (ISBNs) for the Work.

Electronic download/diskette:_____
Rocket Edition:

VI. Advertising and Promotions

A. Publisher shall have the right to use the author's name or pseudonym, likeness, and biographical material for any reasonable advertisement, publication, promotion of the Work itself, its title and all material.

B. Publisher retains the right to determine the type, time, method, place and manner of advertising and promotion, except as agreed to in writing signed by both Author and Publisher.

C. Publisher shall send at least three (3) advance copies of work out for review. Publisher will also provide Author with galleys and/or diskette of the final, approved version of the Work, which may be used by Author to make additional review copies. Author agrees to share with Publisher copies of reviews received; and Publisher likewise agrees to same.

D. Publisher will provide Author with at least one (1) copy of art and/or other promotional material that may be copied and/or distributed at conferences, signings, mailing, etc.

E. Author may not copy or sell copies of Work other than those procured through Publisher. Author may purchase any number of electronic format books for Author's resale use at conferences, signings, local booksellers, etc., at full price from Publisher, and will receive royalties on said purchase. Any other sales must be through Publisher or Publisher-approved vendor.

F. If Author has a website, Author may use up to three chapters of the final, approved version of the Work as a promotional teaser on website. Author's website must include a link to Publisher's website.

G. Publisher will promote the Work though its website for the term of the contract, as well as other promotions such as via Internet, mailings, press and news releases, and miscellaneous advertising.

VII. Term of Contract

A. The term of this Contract is twelve (12) months, and will be perpetually renewed on the anniversary date of initial publication of electronic version of Work unless Author or Publisher cancels Contract in writing at least fifteen (15) days prior to anniversary date. Any such notification of intention to terminate contract is to be delivered by certified mail or other receipted delivery service. Initial publication date shall be set forth in writing by Publisher within thirty (30) days of intended date of publication.

B. During term of Contract, the Work will not be said to be "out of print" and will be available for purchase and distribution after initial publication date.

C. Upon breach of contract, Contract may be terminated by either party with a 30-day notice. Notification of breach and intention to terminate contract is to be delivered by certified mail or other receipted delivery service. If breaching party corrects breach within the 30 days, the Contract shall continue to remain in place until its natural expiration. Upon expiration of Contract term, all rights granted to Publisher will then return to Author at such time.

D. At termination of Contract, Author will be given the opportunity to any part of inventory at 10% above cost without royalty compensation. If Author declines opportunity, Publisher retains the right to sell any outstanding inventory. Author will receive the standard applicable royalty on these copies.

VIII. Miscellaneous

A. **Audit** Author may, with reasonable notice, assign and designate a representative to examine Publisher's records as relate to the Work. Such examination shall be at Author's expense unless errors are found in excess of 5% of royalties in Author's favor; in which case, Publisher shall then defray all usual, customary, and reasonable charges for such audit. Publisher shall pay Author any sums due within thirty (30) days.

B. **Authors** Whenever the term "Author" refers to more than one person, such persons shall be jointly and severally responsible for all aspects of this Contract.

C. **Bankruptcy** If Publisher should file for bankruptcy or reorganization, or Publisher liquidates its business for any reason, Author may terminate this Contract within sixty (60) days by giving written notice through receipted mail. All rights granted by Author to Publisher will at that time revert back to Author. At such time as Publisher declares bankruptcy proceedings through Chapter 11 or takes other steps prior to actual Chapter 7 declaration, Author may terminate contract with all rights reverting to Author.

D. **Severability** If any part of this Contract is determined by a Court to be unenforceable, the rest of the Contract is still considered to be in force.

IX. Entire Agreement
This Contract hereby constitutes the entire agreement between Author and Publisher, and may not be altered, terminated, or amended except by a writing or addenda executed by all parties named herein.

______________________________ ______________________________

Signature *Date* *Signature* *Date*

Social Security or
Tax ID Number ______________

Colleen Gleason Schulte
Chief Administrative Officer
Avid Press, LLC

Please be advised that this contract is only a sample.
To view it in its actual size visit: www.avidpress.com

SAMPLE (Fig. 5.1)

(Website Business)

Roses Are READ Productions

"Literature in full bloom..."

- ROSES ARE READ PRODUCTIONS
- EVENTS & SIGNINGS
- ABOUT VALERIE ROSE
- NATIONAL BLACK STUDENT UNION CONFERENCE
- LATEST RELEASE
- THE BOOKS YOU'VE BEEN WAITING FOR!
- THE ROSES ARE READ BOOK LIST
- HOW TO ORDER
- WHAT PEOPLE ARE SAYING
- YOU BETTER RECOGNIZE!

Roses Are READ Productions

Roses Are READ is a literary production company based in St. Paul, Minnesota. Valerie Rose is the CEO and the author of several books.

Mission Statement

Our mission is multi-dimensional. We wish to promote reading through the production of high quality books of all types. It is also our mission to feature people of color as the primary characters in these books, as it is our goal to give communities of color the opportunity to see themselves in print, as well as to reflect a true and realistic image to the rest of the reading public.

The above, however, is but one aspect of a plan that encompasses a scope that is much more far-reaching, and has a much higher purpose. The ultimate goal is to impart knowledge, bring joy...and thereby make the world a better place to live.

This knowledge will manifest itself on many different subjects, on many different levels and in many different forms. This knowledge will do one or more of the following:

- Encourage, empower and give hope to those who have lost hope.
- Introduce to some, and to others, re-introduce the concept of One Spirit and The Higher Self.
- Strike a cord and capture public attention with a bold, new voice.
- Educate, captivate, motivate, inspire and uplift both adults and children alike.
- Touch, move and change people's lives.
- Encourage people to live life to the fullest without fear.
- Serve humanity by being a positive force in the Universe.
- Foster peace and peace of mind.
- Blossom and grow.
- Entertain. For to entertain, is to delight. And to delight, is to bring joy. And to bring joy is to make the world a better place to live.

SAMPLE (FIG. 5.1A)

(Website Business, cont.)

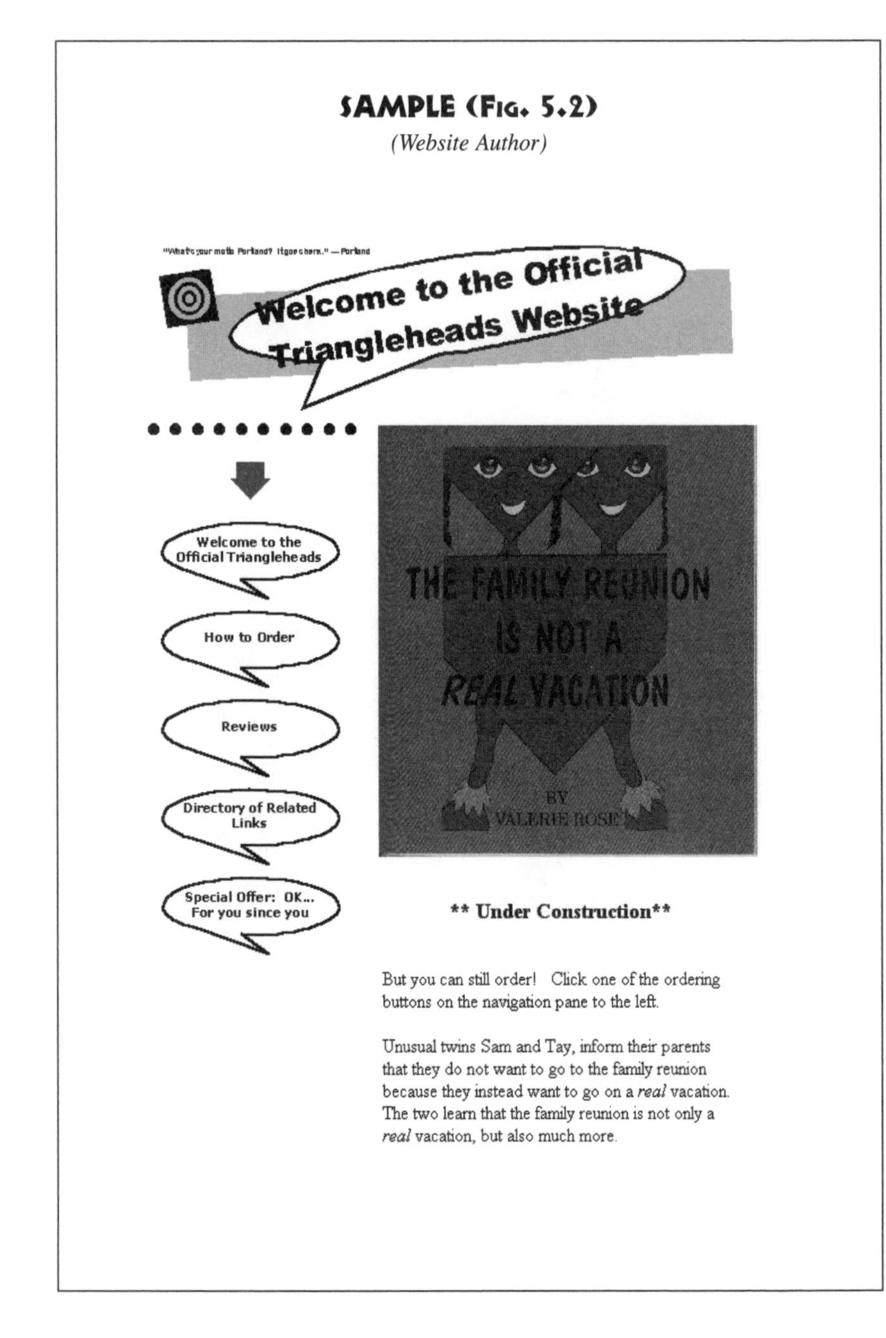

SAMPLE (Fig. 5.2)

(Website Author)

SAMPLE (FIG. 5.3)

(Website Book)

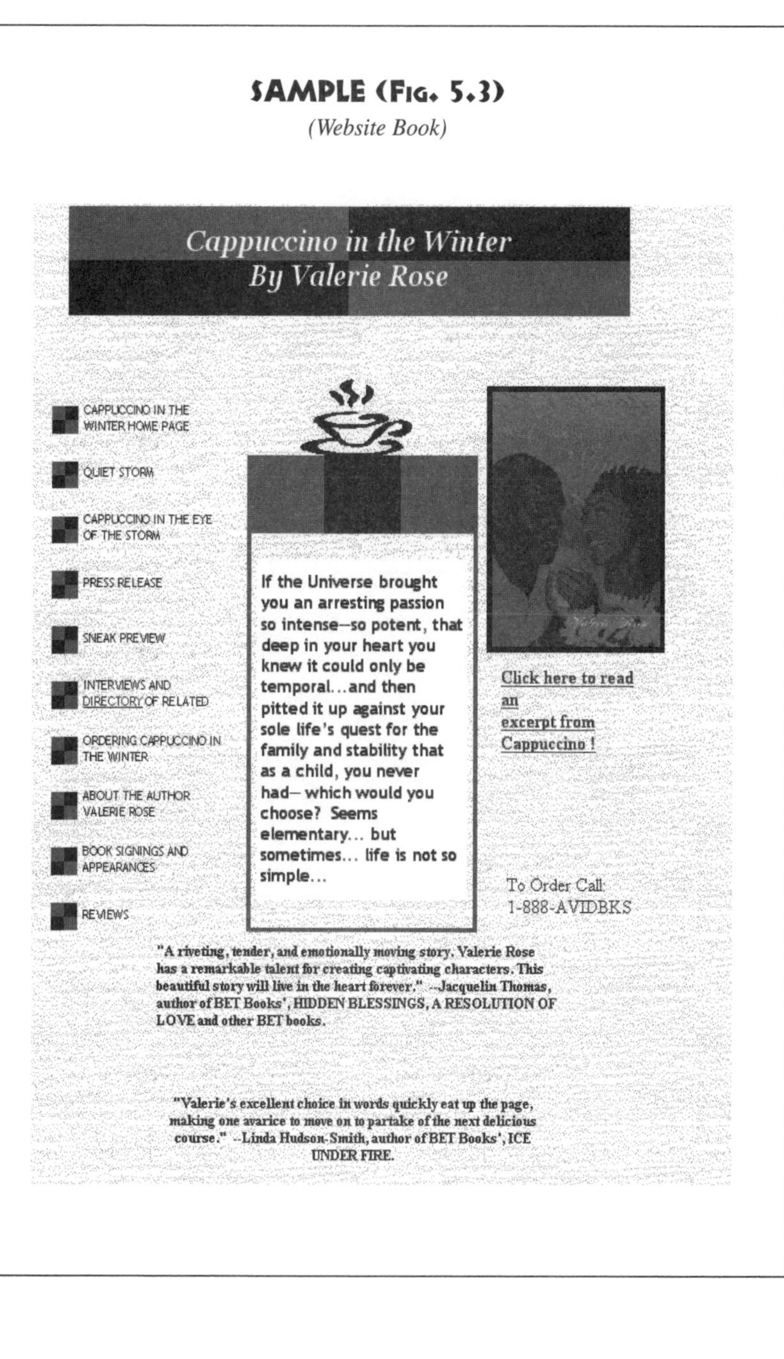

SAMPLE (Fig. 6.1)

(Order Form)

Roses Are READ Productions Presents

Roses are READ

The Books You've Been Waiting For!

Valerie Rose
lives in Minneapolis, Minnesota with her two daughters.

You Better Recognize!

Life is a trip! Literally. Life is a trip! It's a spiritual journey. *You Better Recognize!* is a spiritual guide and a lessons-learned toolkit to help you to start recognizing the joy and power within.

$14.95
$18.95 Canada

Dream Your Dream: Getting Your Writing Out There!

You've always dreamed of writing the great American novel. But how do you start? Where do you start? What is the writing process? How do you structure a compelling story? What tools should you use? Should you go the traditional publishing route or self-publish? How do you obtain a copyright?

Dream Your Dream: Getting Your Writing Out There! is a quick reference guide that delivers a unique, multi-dimensional approach to helping you to answer these questions and more.

$15.00
$19.00 Canada

Cappuccino in the Winter

An arresting passion causes sparks to fly when a computer virus expert teams up with a former hacker to catch a desperate cyberthief.

$6.50
$8.50 Canada

To order by phone call: 1-888-284-325

The Family Reunion is Not a Real Vacation

Unusual twins Sam and Tay, inform their parents that they do not want to go to the family reunion because they instead want to go on a real vacation. The two learn that the family reunion is not only a real vacation, but also much more.

$9.95
$12.95 Canada

ORDER FORM

Mail your check or money order with this completed order form to:

Roses Are READ Productions
Attn: Valerie Rose
P.O. Box 7844
St. Paul, MN 55107
e-mail: valerie.rose@gte.net
websites: *www.valerierose.com* or *www.rosesareread.cc*
www.thetriangleheads.com

QTY.	PRICE	BOOK	TOTAL
	$14.95	*You Better Recognize!*	
	$15.00	*Dream Your Dream: Getting Your Writing Out There!*	
	$ 6.50	*Cappuccino in the Winter*	
	$ 9.95	*The Family Reunion is Not a Vacation*	
		Sub Total	
		Sales Tax *(6.5% Minnesota Residents)*	
		Shipping *($3.00 per shipment / $1.50 per item)*	
		Total	

Name: ______________________

Address: ______________________

City: ____________ State: ________ Zip: ________

Phone: ____________ E-mail: ____________

Published by Beaver's Pond Press and Roses are READ Productions of St.Paul, Minnesota.

SAMPLE (FIG. 6.2)

(Business Card)

Roses Are READ Productions

Literature in full bloom...

Valerie Rose

President/CEO

P. O. Box 7844
St. Paul, MN 55107

Phone: (651)123-4567
E-mail: valerie.rose@gte.net
Website: www.valerierose.com
Website: www.rosesareread.cc

SAMPLE (FIG. 6.3)

(First Sale)

Memorandum

To: Gerri Smith
From: Valerie Rose
Date: 3/3/02
Re: First Sale

Valerie Rose is pleased to announce the sale of her first book length piece, Cappuccino in the Winter. Avid Press chose Cappuccino in the Winter to launch their new Kismet line. This creative work of fiction is part of Avid's Grand Opening in the fall and is scheduled for release in print, electronic, and rocket formats in October 1999.

CONFIDENTIAL

Valerie was the featured artist on Write On Radio! Write On Radio is a radio program which airs weekly on KFAI FM and features readings, performances, and interviews by and with locally, nationally, and internationally known writers. In a segment called, AN ONGOING CONVERSATION, moderator, J.Otis Powell!, interviewed Valerie following the reading of her creative non-fiction piece entitled: WRITING AND RACE: INTEGRITY AND CONCESSIONS, which is to appear in The View Magazine, a publication of the Loft Literary Center of Minneapolis. Valerie's piece, is one of a series of articles about the conjunction of writing and race.

SAMPLE (Fig. 7.1)

(Cover Art Contract)

Roses Are READ Productions
Contractual Copyright Agreement

This Contract is entered into as of September 15, 2001 by and between

Roses Are READ Productions, a business owned by Valerie Rose and existing under the laws of the State of Minnesota, located at 546 Landcaster Road, Crystal, MN 55281 (hereafter known as the "Author and Originator")

and

Elayne Studios, located in Greenwood, California (hereafter known as the "Artist and Photographer")

Concerning the photographs (hereafter referred to as "The Images") for the work tenatively entitled, You Better Recognize...(hereafter referred to as "The Book").

This Contract is entered into in good faith, and signatures from all parties named herein indicate acceptance and agreement to the terms described herewith. This Contract shall be considered legal and binding in all countries. Should any legal dispute arise, the laws of the State of Minnesota shall be applied in any legal action involving such disputes shall take place in the State of Minnesota.

I. Grant of Rights

The "Artist and Photographer" agrees to grant the "Author and Originator" and assigns, the right and permission to use and publish, in any form, including print and electronic, "The Images", without charge, for utilization as the cover art for "The Work". The "Artist and Photographer" agrees to provide the "Author and Originator" with photographs of "The Images". The "Artist and Photographer" understands that "The Images" would be scanned and imported into a graphic design software product like PageMaker or Quark Xpress, and merged with text, to create a cover image for "The Work". The "Artist and Photographer" agrees that "The Images" may also be used to promote "The Work" in publications, audio-visual presentations, promotional literature, television appearances, advertising, web sites, or in any other manner. "The Artist and Photographer" further agrees that this proposal is a promotional opportunity. The "Artist and Photographer" agrees that no monies, including fees, royalties, and/or residuals from "The Work", now or in the future, will be received, charged or exchanged for the granting of this right. Instead, "The Author and Originator" agrees to include a black and white page (which is consistent with the rest of the paging) in "The Work" that would credit "The Artist and Photographer" for the art that appears on the cover, and list along with a brief bio, an associated address and web site. "The Artist and Photographer" agrees that the rights granted above apply world wide.

II. Term of Contract

This contract shall never expire.

III. Entire Agreement

This Contract hereby constitutes the entire agreement between the Author and Originator and the Artist and Photographer, and may not be altered, terminated, or amended, except in writing or addenda executed by all parties named herein.

______________________	__________	______________________	__________
Signature	Date	Signature	Date

Kurt Elayne
Elayne Studios, Inc.

Valerie Rose
Roses Are Read Productions

SAMPLE (FIG. 7.2)

(Photo Release)

Photo Release

I, ____

Hereby give Valerie Rose, her legal representatives and assigns, the right and permission to publish, without charge, photographs taken by me on at 546 Landcaster Road, Crystal, MN 55281. These pictures may be used in publications, audio-visual presentations, promotional literature, advertising, or in any other manner. I hereby warrant that I , Henry Jackson, am over eighteen (18) years of age, and am competent to contract in my own name so far as the above is concerned. Photographer's

Signature________________________________

Date________________________________

Address________________________________

City________________________________

State_______________ ZIP_______________

Telephone________________________________

SAMPLE (FIG. 7.3)

(Model Release)

Model Release

I, ____

Hereby give Valerie Rose, her legal representatives and assigns, the right and permission to publish, without charge, photographs of me taken on August 15, 1999________________________
At 546 Landcaster Road, Crystal, MN 55281______________
These pictures may be used in publications, audio-visual presentations, promotional literature, advertising, or in any other manner. I hereby warrant that I , Karen Kensington, am over eighteen (18) years of age, and am competent to contract in my own name so far as the above is concerned.

Model's Signature_________________________________

Date____

Address____

City______________________State________Zip__________

Telephone____

SAMPLE (FIG. 8.1)

(Press Release)

Press Release

FOR IMMEDIATE RELEASE
Story Date: April 12, 2000

For Further Information Contact:
Valerie Rose at valerie.rose@gte.net

Local Author Leverages Power of Technology to Make Dream Come True

Minneapolis, MN – April 12, 2000 -- Introduced to the internet by a friend back when the Internet was still new, Valerie Rose of Minneapolis, Minnesota has since leveraged its power to inch by inch move her dream of having her novel published into reality. Set in the frigid Twin Cities of Minneapolis/St. Paul, *CAPPUCCINO IN THE WINTER* is Rose's debut novel. And despite its decidedly frigid setting, it was recommended by Midwestwoman.com as one of the 10 Best Beach Books.

Avid Press Chooses Valerie Rose's Debut Novel to Launch its New Kismet Line

Started by two sisters in Brighton, Michigan, Avid Press wants to bring fresh new fiction to Avid Readers. "We love Valerie's book!" exclaims publisher, Colleen Gleason Schulte. "We really like the story, the characters and the very realistic, well-rounded plot," adds sister, Kate Gleason. "Valerie's smooth flowing description defies dictionary depiction. Her excellent choice in words quickly eat up the page, making one avarice to move on to partake of the next delicious course," raves Linda Hudson-Smith, author of BET Books', ICE UNDER FIRE.

Valerie Rose is the Featured Guest on Milwaukee Public Television

"I've always wanted to write a book, but it was always sort of a nebulous dream out there," Valerie tells interviewer, Liddy Collins of Milwaukee Public Television. "I always thought it was something other people do. But then I realized that I am other people!"

Valerie Rose is the Featured Artist on Write On! Radio

"Yes, I am extremely happy to have my book published," Valerie tells radio moderator, J.Otis Powell! of KFAI radio, "but that was a direct result of having a presence on the internet. For writers, you have to have a presence on the internet because if you don't, you are operating at a huge disadvantage because there's a wealth of information out there that's just waiting at your fingertips to access."

A native of Milwaukee, Wisconsin, Valerie has lived in the Twin Cities for twelve years. She is an author, essayist and poet with work in The Minneapolis Spokesman, Futures Magazine, The View (from the Loft), The St. Paul Recorder and Jive Magazine. She is a member of The Midwest Fiction Writers, The Loft Literary Center of Minneapolis, and The Romance Writers of America. For more information on Rose's book, to be placed on her mailing list, or to inquire about interviews, write, call or e-mail her with your request.

Interview Contact:

Attn: Valerie Rose
P.O. Box 7844
St. Paul, MN 55107
(000) 555-5555 (D) (000) 555-5555 (E)
e-mail: valerie.rose@gte.net
website: www.valerierose.com

Title Details:

CAPPUCCINO IN THE WINTER
by Valerie Rose
Release Date: December, 1999
ISBNs:
Print: 1-929613-08-3
Electronic: 1-929613-06-7
RocketEdition: 1-929613-07-5
Avid Press website: http://www.avidpress.com/

SAMPLE (FIG. 8.2)

(Review Sheet)

REVIEWS

Cappuccino in the Winter
by Valerie Rose

"A riveting, tender, and emotionally moving story. Valerie Rose has a remarkable talent for creating captivating characters. This beautiful story will live in the heart forever."

—Jacquelin Thomas, author of BET Books', HIDDEN BLESSINGS.

"Valerie's excellent choice in words quickly eat up the page, making one avarice to move on to partake of the next delicious course."

—Linda Hudson-Smith, author of BET Books', ICE UNDER FIRE.

"CAPPUCCINO IN THE WINTER focuses on two very sensitive human emotions, the trauma of the foster child, and the impact of adultery on the innocent mate. The reader enters the cyber world of computers; the plot is littered with intrigue. This novel would set a movie screen ablaze with action, romance and drama."

—Rendezvous Magazine

"Cappuccino in the Winter steams with unquenchable passion and subterfuge. Take a sip and I promise you won't be able to put it down until the very last drop.

—Rick Malone, author of Violet of a Deeper Blue

"An exciting tale of corporate politics, romance, and a bit of political intrigue. Here is a book that will call for your undivided attention as the book begins with a bang and only picks up its pace from there! I find myself looking forward to the next story by Valerie Rose! " ***

—HUNTRESS BOOK REVIEWS
(Reviewed by Détra Fitch)

"...CAPPUCCINO IN THE WINTER will delight both computer aficionados and romance fans."

—www.romanceincolor.com

Print:	1-929613-08-3
Electronic:	1-929613-06-7
RocketEdition:	1-929613-07-5

SAMPLE (FIG. 8.3)

(Review Sheet)

Reviews

The Family Reunion
Is Not A *Real*
Vacation

Written by
Valerie Rose
and
Illustrated by
Samuel J. Simmons

Unusual twins Sam and Tay, inform their parents that they do not want to go to the family reunion because they instead want to go on a *real* vacation. The two learn that the family reunion is not only a *real* vacation, but also much more.

"A WONDERFUL BOOK...INSIGHTFUL...A book for all ages, espousing the virtues and fun of the time honored family reunion."
— Ken Burkeen, Book Channel Manager, BlackVoices.com

"An entertaining way of teaching children to value family."
—F.M. Avey, author *The Harlequin's Nutcracker, Girl Gifts*

"In just a few short pages, The Family Reunion Is Not A *Real* Vacation took me down memory lane to my own family reunion as a child and as an adult. Valerie Rose connected the dots in showing children how family reunions truly can be a real vacation."
—Sandra King Freeman, Soulful Crosswords

"I think this is a good book for kids to read. It teaches us that it is important and fun to spend time with our family."
—Marlon Watts, Children's Book Reviewer
The Hook Up Network (TheHUNetwork)
Empowerment Zone (e-Zone) Newsletter.

Published by Beaver's Pond Press in association with Roses Are READ Productions

ISBN: 1-931646-00-7 Visit us online at: www.thetriangleheads.com

SAMPLE (Fig. 9.1)

(Promo Sheet)

THE FAMILY REUNION IS NOT A REAL VACATION

Written by
Valerie Rose
and
Illustrated by
Samuel J. Simmons

Unusual twins Sam and Tay Trianglehead, after discovering the travel vacation plans of their friends, the Ovalheads and Triangleheads, inform their parents that they do not want to go to their family reunion because they instead want to go on a *real* vacation. The two learn that the family reunion is not only a *real* vacation, but also much more. Beautifully illustrated, this book uniquely and simultaneously, educates kids on geometric shapes, colors, numbers, geography, culture, family and productive problem resolution.

Published by Beaver's Pond Press in association with Roses Are READ Productions

ISBN: 1-931646-00-7 Visit us online at: www.thetriangleheads.com

SAMPLE (FIG. 9.2)

(Cappucino Promo Sheet)

Cappuccino in the Winter
By
Valerie Rose

*** Set in the Twin Cities ***

SHE WILL DO ANYTHING TO REACH HER DREAM

Computer security expert Alayna Alexander will do anything to have a family--including marry a man that she doesn't love. Warren Harrington will give her the family she craves, despite the fact that he does not spark her deepest passions.

SHE'LL GIVE UP LOVE TO HAVE A FAMILY

But confusion in the form of tall, dark Khavon Brighton, a former computer hacker, slips into Alayna's life when she is assigned to work with him on a top-level computer security project. Sparks fly as the two race to thwart a desperate cyberthief who has a personal vendetta against Khavon.

WILL PASSION WIN OUT?

From a corporate world of greed and intrigue...through the perils of Minnesota snowstorms...to the titillating city of Amsterdam, Khavon and Alayna fight a passion that won't be subdued as they expose a far-reaching, devious plot.

***** Sneak Preview *****

"Are you trying to tell me that you want out?" Alik said, his eyes blazing murderously into Trojan's. "Is that what this is about?"

Trojan's face grew pensive. He slowly nodded his head. "It's just that I didn't realize——"

"No. No need to explain. I understand. You want out of the KGB," he said through a thick accent. "Simple enough. The choice is yours. The choice is and has always been yours. But before you go, I have something that I think may be of interest to you."

Trojan stood rigid with terror as Alik Ivanov moved to open his top right desk drawer. The blood pounding in his ears subsided into an involuntary sigh of relief when Alik handed him a manila envelope.

"I understand it's been some time since you've heard from your friend Ravenger. There's a reason for that."

Eyes transfixed with horror, Trojan stared at the photograph of his friend lying in a crimson pool of blood, his neck slashed.

Ivanov ran a cavalier hand over his slick black hair. "He wanted out too."

***

Alayna gave him a once-over, her dark eyebrows raised with much attitude. "Okay, I guess you just didn't hear me when I said that I was engaged."

"Yeah, I heard you. But does he treat you like the Nubian queen that you are?"

Taken by surprise, Alayna felt her heart stop momentarily. His voice, like deep, dark, chocolate syrup, was smooth and rich. His insightful discernment was inexplicably accurate. His words, spoken so nonchalantly, made her question if he had really said them or not. But if he did, she most definitely wanted to hear them again . . .

To order, call 1-888-AVIDBKS (284-3257) or Visit www.avidpress.com

SAMPLE (FIG. 9.3)

(Booksigning Flyer)

Book Signing

Meet Twin Cities' Own
Valerie Rose

Signing her new book
"Cappuccino in the Winter"

Friday, September 29th from 5-7 PM
Mall of America
Barnes and Noble

Set in the Twin Cities! From a corporate world of greed and intrigue... through the perils of Minnesota snowstorms... to the titillating city of Amsterdam, former computer hacker, Khavon Brighton and computer security expert, Alayna Alexander fight a passion that won't be subdued as they chase a cyberthief and end up exposing a far-reaching, devious plot !

"A riveting, tender, and emotionally moving story. Valerie Rose has a remarkable talent for creating captivating characters. This beautiful story will live in the heart forever."
—Jacquelin Thomas, author of BET Books', HIDDEN BLESSINGS.

"Valerie's excellent choice in words quickly eat up the page, making one avarice to move on to partake of the next delicious course."
—Linda Hudson-Smith, author of BET Books', ICE UNDER FIRE.

Cappuccino in the Winter steams with unquenchable passion and subterfuge.
Take a sip and I promise you won't be able to put it down until the very last drop.
—Rick Malone, author of Violet of a Deeper Blue

"An exciting tale of corporate politics, romance, and a bit of political intrigue. Here is a book that will call for your undivided attention as the book begins with a bang and only picks up its pace from there! I find myself looking forward to the next story by Valerie Rose! " *** —HUNTRESS BOOK REVIEWS

SAMPLE (Fig. 9.4)

(Advertisement)

The Family Reunion Is Not A Real Vacation

By Valerie Rose

Unusual twins Sam and Tay, inform their parents that they do not want to go to the family reunion because they instead want to go on a *real* vacation. The two learn that the family reunion is not only a *real* vacation, but also much more.

Makes a great Christmas gift!!

"AWONDERFUL BOOK…INSIGHTFUL…A book for all ages espousing the virtues and fun of the time honored family reunion."
—Ken Burkeen
Book Channel Manager,
BlackVoices.com

Regularly $12.95, but mention this ad and get it for only $10.00!

Visit **www.thetriangleheads.com** and mail your check or money order with the completed order form to:

Roses Are READ Productions
Attn: Valerie Rose
P. O. Box 7844
St. Paul, MN 55107
- or -
e-mail Valerie Rose at:
valerie.rose @gte.net;

Visit www.valerierose.com

Visit www.thetriangleheads.com * ISBN: 1-931646-00-7

SAMPLE (FIG. 9.5)

(Sell Sheet)

There is this light, this power within.
It's there, but we don't *recognize* it.

A Spiritual Guide -
Because Life's A "Trip"

Life is a "trip." Literally, life is a "trip." It is a spiritual journey. It's a wild and perplexing ride, where sometimes we cruise through blissfully under sunny, blue skies and then other times we are left to navigate the rough terrain of confusing twists and turns. If the road of life has you lost and you find yourself going around in circles, stop and seek some direction. Pick up this guide and start recognizing the light, the joy and the power within.

Now Available!

Visit us online at:

www.rosesareread.cc www.valerierose.com

The latest release from:

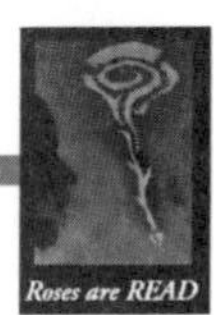

PRODUCTIONS

ISBN: 1-931646-22-8

SAMPLE (Fig. 9.6)

(Artistic Experience)

Artistic Experience - Valerie Rose

Publisher/Literary Event	Experience	Date/Venue
Cooley Family Reunion President Casino, Buloxi, MS	Book Signing	May 24, 2002
Montsho Books, Orlando Florida	Book Signing	May 23, 2002
Cultural Connection Bookstore Milwaukee, Wisconsin	Book Signing	May 18, 2002
Our Story Bookstore Plainfield, NJ	Book Signing	May 4, 2002
University of Wisconsin-Whitewater's African American Heritage Lecture Series	**Valerie was one in the list of distinguished speakers that included, Wisconsin Senator: Gary George, Jazz Musician: Manty Ellis, and Milwaukee Journal/Sentinel Columnist: Eugene Kane.**	**March 2002**
Romance Slam Jam 2002	Appearance/Workshop Facilitation **Cappuccino sold out**	March 2002
UMBA Book Festival	Featured Author/Signing with Midwest Fiction Writers and Beaver's Pond Press	September 2001 St. Paul, Minnesota
Congressional Black Caucus Foundation	**Guest Author in the Authors Pavilion**	**September 2001 Washington, D. C.**
Author's Symposium National Black MBA Association	Panelist	September 2001
The Gathering: Women of Color Minneapolis Convention Center	Featured Author; Book Signing Second appearance.	June 2001 Minneapolis
BlackVoices.com	"The Family Reunion Is Not A Real Vacation" hailed by BlackVoices.com book manager, Ken Burkeen, as "A wonderful book...Insightful..."	May 2001
Roses Are READ Productions	"The Family Reunion Is Not A Real Vacation"/Children's book Second Edition	May 2001 Minneapolis
Romance Slam Jam 2001	Appearance **Cappuccino sold out**	March 2001
ABC Radio Network	Interview with DeWayne Dancer and Pam Gibson	February 2001

SAMPLE (Fig. 9.6a)

(Artistic Experience, cont.)

Twin Cities Black Authors Showcase	Book Signing	February 2001
Black Issues Book Review	"Cappuccino in the Winter" ***Recommended new title**	September/October 2000
Shades of Romance Online Magazine Premiere Issue	*Selected as Author of the Month "Olivia's Dream" "From Seed to Harvest" "Tips for New Writers" Interview	September 2000 Internet
Mall of America Barnes and Noble	Book Signing	September 2000 Bloomington, MN
KSGS 950 Solid Gold Soul Freddie Bell Morning Show	Featured Artist/Interview	September 2000 Minneapolis
UMBA Book Festival	Book Signing	September 2000 Minneapolis
KFAI - Write On! Radio	Featured Artist/Reading	September 2000 Minneapolis
Ginko's Coffee House	Reading/Book Signing	September 2000 St. Paul
The Jamaica Observer Tourist Times	***Color Photo Feature**	August 2000 Negril, Jamaica
Book Tour (Mini-Tour)	Book Signing ***Sold out at Fairlane Mall**	August 2000 Detroit/Flint
Midwestwoman.com	***At number four, Cappuccino is recommended as one of the 10 top beach books by Midwestwoman.com.**	July 2000
Aberdeen, MS	Book Signing	July 2000 Aberdeen, MS
The Gathering: Women of Color Minneapolis Convention Center	Featured Author; Book Signing	June 2000 Minneapolis
Beaches Inn	Book Signing	June 2000 Negril, Jamaica
East Hilton	Book Signing	May 2000 Memphis, TN
Roses Are READ Productions	"The Triangleheads and The Family Reunion Is Not A Real Vacation"/Children's book First Edition	May 2000 Minneapolis
Walden Books (Ridgedale Mall)	Panelist Book Signing	March 2000 Minneapolis
Milwaukee Public Television Black Nouveau Premier News Magazine Program	Featured Artist	March 2000 Milwaukee

SAMPLE (FIG. 9.6B)

(Artistic Experience, cont.)

A View (from the Loft)	"The Literary Divide"	March 2000 Minneapolis
3M Black History Month Cultural Showcase	Book Signing	February 2000 St. Paul
Minnesota Monthly Magazine	Featured Artist Interview	February 2000 Minneapolis
Women's Expo Minneapolis Convention Center	Book Signing	January 2000 Minneapolis
Walden Books (Rosedale Mall)	Book Signing	January 2000 Minneapolis
A View (from the Loft)	"Writing and Race: Integrity vs. Concessions"/Nonfiction Article	November 1999 Minneapolis
Online Writer's Conference	Interview "From Seed to Harvest" "Tips for New Writers"	October 1999 Internet
Futures Magazine	"Olivia's Dream" Short Story	Oct/Nov 1999 Minneapolis
Avid Press	"Cappuccino in the Winter" Novel	October 1999 Michigan
UMBA Book Festival	Appearance	September 1999 Minneapolis
Write On! Radio	Featured Artist/Reading	August 1999 Minneapolis
Futures Magazine	"In a Word" Poem	June/July 1999 Minneapolis
Black Secrets	"Jilted Love" Short Story	November 1998 New York
Jive Magazine	"Saying Goodbye" Short Story	October 1998 New York
Minneapolis Spokesman/ St. Paul Recorder	"Cyberspace or Bust" Nonfiction Article	January 1996 Minneapolis/St. Paul
Black Data Processing Journal	"Network Fellowship" Nonfiction Article	Winter 1989/90 New York

SAMPLE (FIG. 9.7)

(Curricula Vita)

Curriculum Vita

Valerie Rose
529 Landcaster Road
Crystal, MN 55232
(612) 454-3334 (D)
(612) 392-3838 (E)

Curriculum Vita

Title of Piece	Type	Publisher
"Network Fellowship"	Nonfiction Article	Black Data Processing Journal Winter 1989/90 New York
"Cyberspace or Bust"	Nonfiction Article	Minneapolis Spokesman January 25, 1996 Minneapolis
"Cyberspace or Bust"	Nonfiction Article	St. Paul Recorder January 25, 1996 St.Paul
"Saying Goodbye"	Short Story	Jive Magazine October 1998 New York
"Jilted Love"	Short Story	Black Secrets November 1998 New York
"In a Word"	Poem	Futures Magazine June/July 1999 Minneapolis
"Cappuccino in the Winter"	Novel	Avid Press October 1999 Michigan
"Olivia's Dream"	Short Story	Futures Magazine October/November 1999 Minneapolis
"Writing and Race: Integrity vs. Concessions"	Nonfiction Article	A View (from the Loft) November 1999 Minneapolis

SAMPLE (FIG. 10.1)

(Media Kit Checklist)

Valerie Rose

- ❑ **Requested Material label affixed**
- ❑ Reviews
- ❑ Aout the Author - Website4, page 3
- ❑ Card
- ❑ Press Release
- ❑ Cover Letter
- ❑ Photograph
- ❑ Cyberspace or Bust
- ❑ Brochure
- ❑ Bookmark
- ❑ Rocket Flyer
- ❑ Return SASE little envelope included
  - ❑ stamped
  - ❑ signed
  - ❑ labeled
- ❑ Return SASE big envelope included
  - ❑ stamped
  - ❑ signed
  - ❑ labeled

  Postcard included
  - ❑ stamped
  - ❑ labeled
- ❑ Business Card included
- ❑ Cover letter included, all names correct
  - ❑ signed
  - ❑ correct names
- ❑ Synopsis included
- ❑ Three Chapter included
- ❑ Manuscript Rubberbanded
- ❑ Linen Envelope for coverletter,synopsis,checklist
- ❑ Editor Reply Checklist included
- ❑ Pocket File folder to put 3 chapters in/ with rubberbands.
- ❑ Press Release
- ❑ Bio
- ❑ Brochure
- ❑ Flyer?
- ❑ About Avid sheet or brochure
- ❑ Avid Cappuccino Excerpt
- ❑ Bookmark
- ❑ To the media letter or to the booksellers
- ❑ Sample Writings
- ❑ Resume
- ❑ Folder cover/label
- ❑ Letters of Recommendation
- ❑ Website print
- ❑ Article/Reviews
- ❑ What people are saying about books by Valerie Rose
- ❑ Brochure

SAMPLE (FIG. 10.2)

(Form Rejection Letter)

January 1, 2002

Dear Writer,

Thank you for the opportunity to review your manuscript. We regret to inform you that it does not meet our needs at this time for the reason(s) listed below:

- ☐ Too long
- ☐ Too short
- ☐ Pacing is too slow
- ☐ No tension between protagonists
- ☐ Does not meet our guidelines
- ☐ Other

We wish you the best of luck in placing your manuscript elsewhere.

Thank you again for your interest.

Sincerely,

The Editors

(This is a fictional form rejection letter. You can tell that it's a form letter because the manuscript is not mentioned by name and the checklist is a dead give away.)

SAMPLE (FIG. 10.3)

(Personal Rejection Letter)

ABC Book Publishing
123 S. France Street
New York, NY 12345

January 1, 2002

Dear Valerie,

Thank you for the opportunity to review your manuscript, *Cappuccino in the Winter*. While the story does include some intriguing elements, we regret to inform you that it does not meet our needs at this time. We have just recently decided to limit our submission intake to nonfiction works.

And just a side note: I really enjoyed the tension between Alayna and Khavon, but you might want to pick up the pacing a bit in the beginning of the book.

We wish you the best of luck in finding a publisher for your work.

Thank you again for your interest.

Sincerely,

Richard Gayle

(This is a fictional rejection letter that is a little more personalized. You can tell that it's a personalized letter because the manuscript and the characters are mentioned by name. Also the editor gave some constructive criticism.)

Appendix G

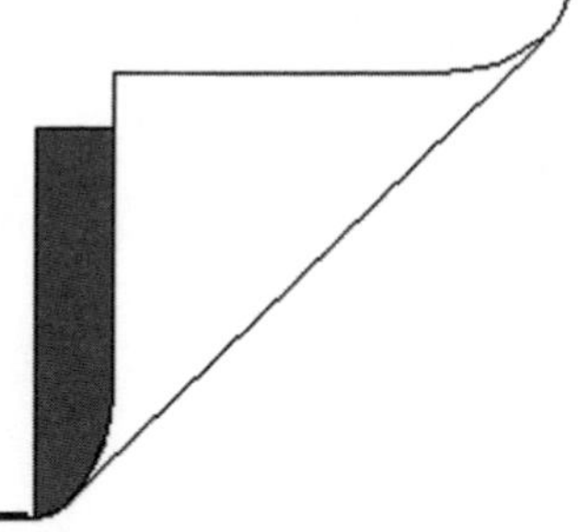

Creating a Marketing Brochure

Cappuccino in the Winter

(Outside of 3-Panel Brochure)

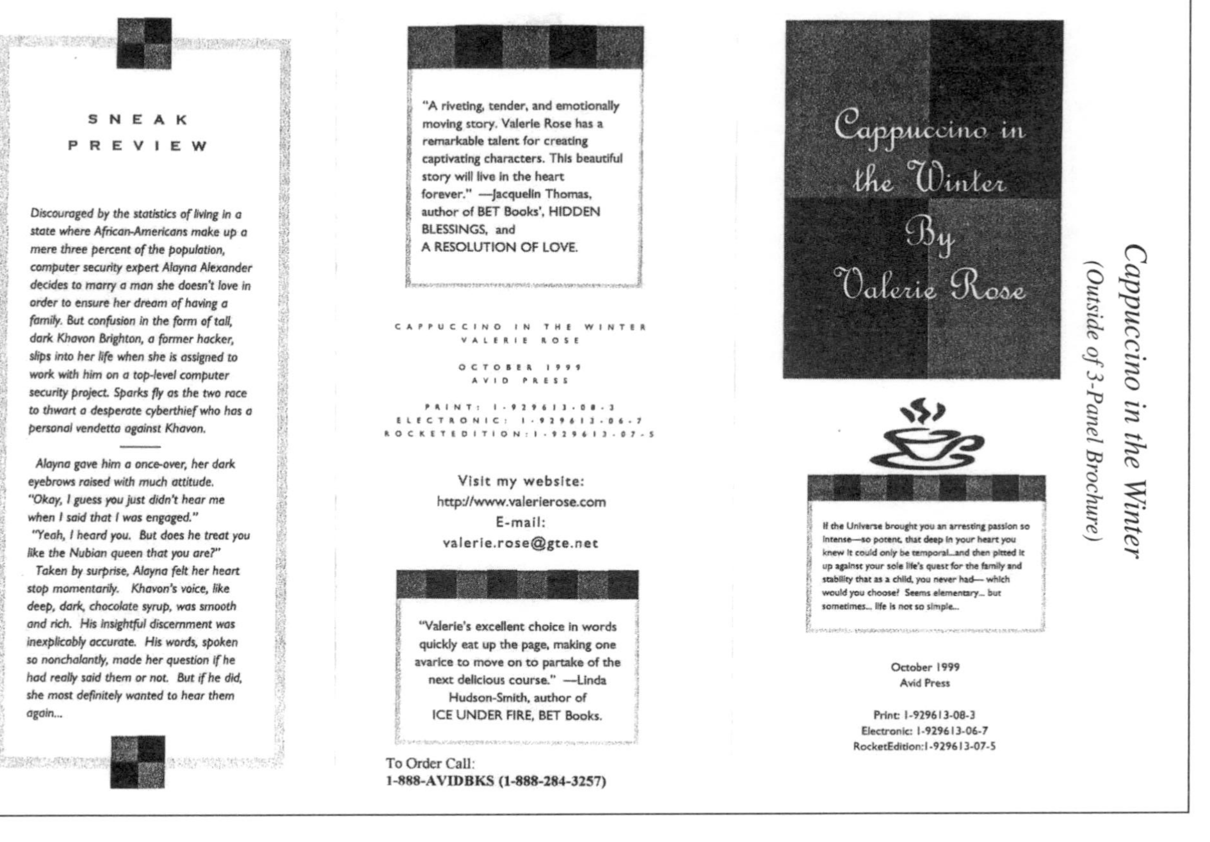

Cappuccino in the Winter

(Inside of 3-Panel Brochure)

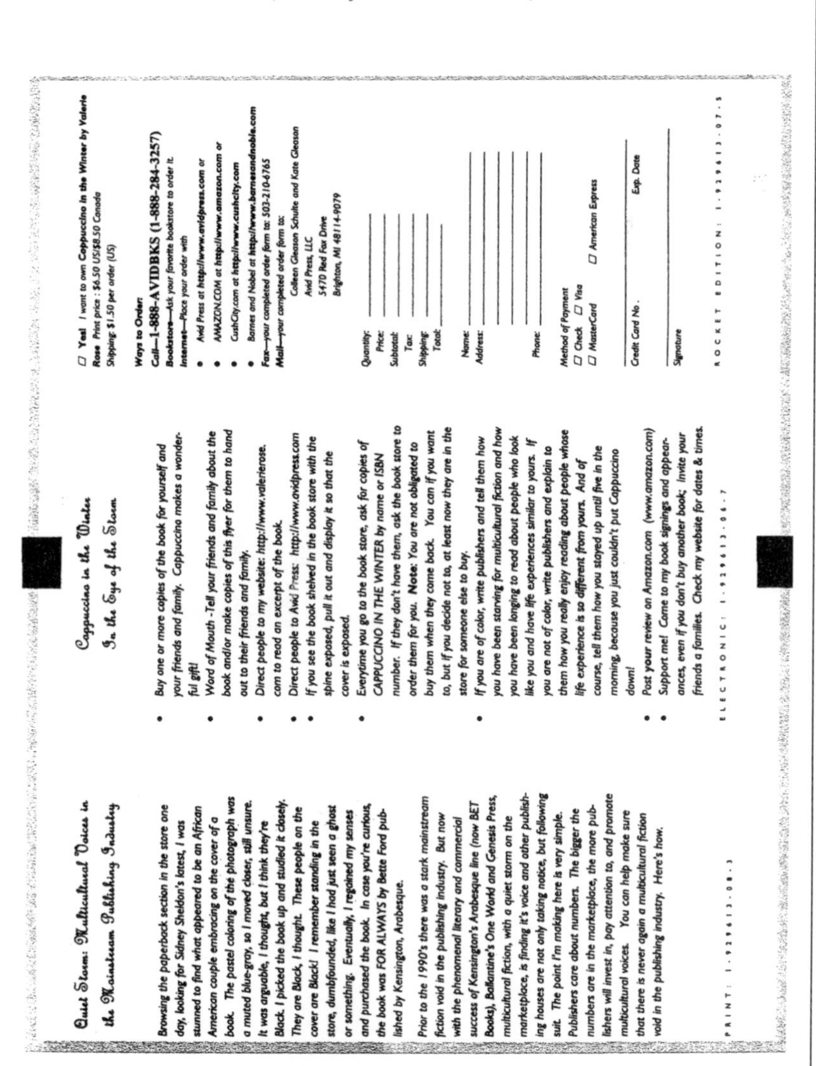

Quiet Storm: Multicultural Voices in the Mainstream Publishing Industry

Browsing the paperback section in the store one day, looking for Sidney Sheldon's latest, I was stunned to find what appeared to be an African American couple embracing on the cover of a book. The pastel coloring of the photograph was a muted blue-gray, so I moved closer, still unsure. It was arguable, I thought, but I think they're Black. I picked the book up and studied it closely. They are Black, I thought. These people on the cover are Black! I remember standing in the store, dumbfounded, like I had just seen a ghost or something. Eventually, I regained my senses and purchased the book. In case you're curious, the book was FOR ALWAYS by Bette Ford published by Kensington, Arabesque.

Prior to the 1990's there was a stark mainstream fiction void in the publishing industry. But now with the phenomenal literary and commercial success of Kensington's Arabesque line (now BET Books), Ballantine's One World and Genesis Press, multicultural fiction, with a quiet storm on the marketplace, is finding it's voice and other publishing houses are not only taking notice, but following suit. The point I'm making here is very simple. Publishers care about numbers. The bigger the numbers are in the marketplace, the more publishers will invest in, pay attention to, and promote multicultural voices. You can help make sure that there is never again a multicultural fiction void in the publishing industry. Here's how.

PRINT: 1-929613-08-3

Cappuccino in the Winter
In the Eye of the Storm

- Buy one or more copies of the book for yourself and your friends and family. Cappuccino makes a wonderful gift!
- Word of Mouth -Tell your friends and family about the book and/or make copies of this flyer for them to hand out to their friends and family.
- Direct people to my website: http://www.valerierose.com to read an excerpt of the book.
- Direct people to Avid Press: http://www.avidpress.com
- If you see the book shelved in the book store with the spine exposed, pull it out and display it so that the cover is exposed.
- Everytime you go to the book store, ask for copies of CAPPUCCINO IN THE WINTER by name or ISBN number. If they don't have them, ask the book store to order them for you. **Note:** You are not obligated to buy them when they come back. You can if you want to, but if you decide not to, at least now they are in the store for someone else to buy.
- If you are of color, write publishers and tell them how you have been starving for multicultural fiction and how you have been longing to read about people who look like you and have life experiences similar to yours. If you are not of color, write publishers and explain to them how you really enjoy reading about people whose life experience is so different from yours. And of course, tell them how you stayed up until five in the morning, because you just couldn't put Cappuccino down!
- Post **your** review on Amazon.com (www.amazon.com)
- Support me! Come to my book signings and appearances, even if you don't buy another book; Invite your friends a families. Check my website for dates & times.

ELECTRONIC: 1-929613-06-7

☐ **Yes!** I want to own **Cappuccino in the Winter by Valerie Rose** Print price : $6.50 US/$8.50 Canada
Shipping: $1.50 per order (US)

Ways to Order:
Call—1-888-AVIDBKS (1-888-284-3257)
Bookstore—Ask your favorite bookstore to order it.
Internet—Place your order with

- Avid Press at **http://www.avidpress.com** or
- AMAZON.COM at **http://www.amazon.com** or
- CushCity.com at **http://www.cushcity.com**
- Barnes and Nobel at **http://www.barnesandnoble.com**

Fax—your completed order form to: 503-210-6765
Mail—your completed order form to:
Colleen Gleason Schulte and Kate Gleason
Avid Press, LLC
5470 Red Fox Drive
Brighton, MI 48114-9079

Quantity: ____________
Price: ____________
Subtotal: ____________
Tax: ____________
Shipping: ____________
Total: ____________

Name: ____________
Address: ____________

Phone: ____________

Method of Payment
☐ Check ☐ Visa
☐ MasterCard ☐ American Express

Credit Card No . ____________ Exp. Date

Signature ____________

ROCKET EDITION: 1-929613-07-5

Brochure Elements

When you are designing a brochure keep it simple.

You want to:

- Inform people about your book.
- Convince them to purchase your book.
- Tell them how they can purchase your book.

Be sure to include the ISBN number, publisher, contact information, and/or an order form.

*On the **cover** page you want to entice people to open the brochure and see what it's about.*

In my brochure I give the reader a ***sneak preview*** *of the book that includes a short synopsis and an excerpt.*

S N E A K

P R E V I E W

Discouraged by the statistics of living in a state where African-Americans make up a mere three percent of the population, computer security expert Alayna Alexander decides to marry a man she doesn't love in order to ensure her dream of having a family. But confusion in the form of tall, dark Khavon Brighton, a former hacker, slips into her life when she is assigned to work with him on a top-level computer security project. Sparks fly as the two race to thwart a desperate cyberthief who has a personal vendetta against Khavon.

Alayna gave him a once-over, her dark eyebrows raised with much attitude. "Okay, I guess you just didn't hear me when I said that I was engaged."

"Yeah, I heard you. But does he treat you like the Nubian queen that you are?"

Taken by surprise, Alayna felt her heart stop momentarily. Khavon's voice, like deep, dark, chocolate syrup, was smooth and rich. His insightful discernment was inexplicably accurate. His words, spoken so nonchalantly, made her question if he had really said them or not. But if he did, she most definitely wanted to hear them again...

I chose to enhance my brochure with ***reviews*** *from other authors. I also included the ISBN number, website, and an e-mail address.*

"A riveting, tender, and emotionally moving story. Valerie Rose has a remarkable talent for creating captivating characters. This beautiful story will live in the heart forever." —Jacquelin Thomas, author of BET Books', HIDDEN BLESSINGS, and A RESOLUTION OF LOVE.

CAPPUCCINO IN THE WINTER
VALERIE ROSE

OCTOBER 1999
AVID PRESS

PRINT: 1-929613-08-3
ELECTRONIC: 1-929613-06-7
ROCKETEDITION: 1-929613-07-5

Visit my website:
http://www.valerierose.com
E-mail:
valerie.rose@gte.net

"Valerie's excellent choice in words quickly eat up the page, making one avarice to move on to partake of the next delicious course." —Linda Hudson-Smith, author of ICE UNDER FIRE, BET Books.

To Order Call:
1-888-AVIDBKS (1-888-284-3257)

*I give the readers **reasons** why they should purchase the book.*

Quiet Storm: Multicultural Voices in the Mainstream Publishing Industry

Browsing the paperback section in the store one day, looking for Sidney Sheldon's latest, I was stunned to find what appeared to be an African American couple embracing on the cover of a book. The pastel coloring of the photograph was a muted blue-gray, so I moved closer, still unsure. It was arguable, I thought, but I think they're Black. I picked the book up and studied it closely. They are Black, I thought. These people on the cover are Black! I remember standing in the store, dumbfounded, like I had just seen a ghost or something. Eventually, I regained my senses and purchased the book. In case you're curious, the book was FOR ALWAYS by Bette Ford published by Kensington, Arabesque.

Prior to the 1990's there was a stark mainstream fiction void in the publishing industry. But now with the phenomenal literary and commercial success of Kensington's Arabesque line (now BET Books), Ballantine's One World and Genesis Press, multicultural fiction, with a quiet storm on the marketplace, is finding it's voice and other publishing houses are not only taking notice, but following suit. The point I'm making here is very simple. Publishers care about numbers. The bigger the numbers are in the marketplace, the more publishers will invest in, pay attention to, and promote multicultural voices. You can help make sure that there is never again a multicultural fiction void in the publishing industry. Here's how.

PRINT: 1-929613-08-3

Here, I give readers ideas on how they can ***support*** *me and my product.*

Cappuccino in the Winter

In the Eye of the Storm

- *Buy one or more copies of the book for yourself and your friends and family. Cappuccino makes a wonderful gift!*
- *Word of Mouth -Tell your friends and family about the book and/or make copies of this flyer for them to hand out to their friends and family.*
- *Direct people to my website: http://www.valerierose.com to read an excerpt of the book.*
- *Direct people to Avid Press: http://www.avidpress.com*
- *If you see the book shelved in the book store with the spine exposed, pull it out and display it so that the cover is exposed.*
- *Everytime you go to the book store, ask for copies of CAPPUCCINO IN THE WINTER by name or ISBN number. If they don't have them, ask the book store to order them for you.* **Note:** *You are not obligated to buy them when they come back. You can if you want to, but if you decide not to, at least now they are in the store for someone else to buy.*
- *If you are of color, write publishers and tell them how you have been starving for multicultural fiction and how you have been longing to read about people who look like you and have life experiences similar to yours. If you are not of color, write publishers and explain to them how you really enjoy reading about people whose life experience is so different from yours. And of course, tell them how you stayed up until five in the morning, because you just couldn't put Cappuccino down!*
- *Post* ***your*** *review on Amazon.com (www.amazon.com)*
- *Support me! Come to my book signings and appearances, even if you don't buy another book; Invite your friends a families. Check my website for dates & times.*

ELECTRONIC: 1-929613-06-7

Also, I included an ***order form*** *to give readers a method of ordering.*

☐ **Yes!** *I want to own* **Cappuccino in the Winter by Valerie Rose** *Print price : $6.50 US/$8.50 Canada*
Shipping: $1.50 per order (US)

Ways to Order:
Call—1-888-AVIDBKS (1-888-284-3257)
Bookstore—*Ask your favorite bookstore to order it.*
Internet—*Place your order with*

- *Avid Press at* **http://www.avidpress.com** *or*
- *AMAZON.COM at* **http://www.amazon.com** *or*
- *CushCity.com at* **http://www.cushcity.com**
- *Barnes and Nobel at* **http://www.barnesandnoble.com**

Fax—*your completed order form to: 503-210-6765*
Mail—*your completed order form to:*

Colleen Gleason Schulte and Kate Gleason
Avid Press, LLC
5470 Red Fox Drive
Brighton, MI 48114-9079

Quantity: ________
Price: ________
Subtotal: ________
Tax: ________
Shipping: ________
Total: ________

Name: ________
Address: ________
____
____
____
Phone: ________

Method of Payment
☐ Check ☐ Visa
☐ MasterCard ☐ American Express

____
Credit Card No . Exp. Date

____
Signature

ROCKET EDITION: 1-929613-07-5

Create a Bookmark

Create a bookmark that you can give away at book signings. Readers love to walk away with something and they will help you advertise your book beyond the event.

Appendix H

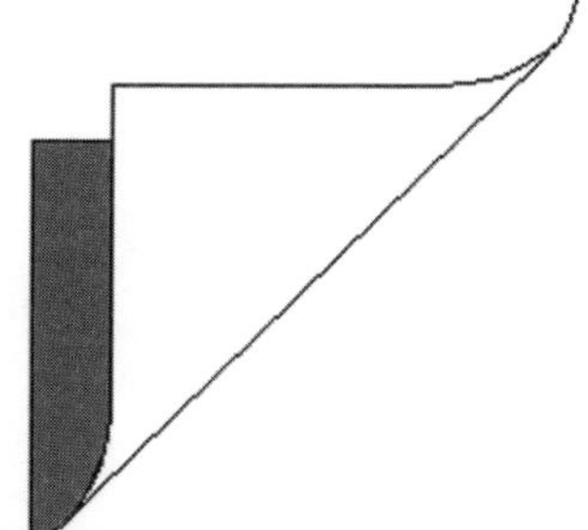

Bibliography

Swain, Dwight V. (1965). *Techniques of the Selling Writer, OK*: University of Oklahoma Press.

Ray, Robert J. (1994). *The Weekend Novelist,* NY: Bantam Doubleday Dell Publishing Group.

McKee, Robert (1997). *Story*, NY: Harper-Collins Publishers.

Bickam, Jack M. (1993). *Scene & Structure*, OH: F&W Publications, Inc.

Conrad, Barnaby (1990). *The Complete Guide to Writing Fiction*, OH: F&W Publications, Inc.

Noble, William (1994). *Conflict, Action & Suspense*, OH: F&W Publications, Inc.

The Writer's Digest (1994). *Guide to Good Writing*, OH: F&W Publications, Inc.

Swain, Dwight V. (1990). *Creating Characters & How to Build Story People*, OH: F&W Publications, Inc.

McCutcheon, Marc (1996). *Building Believable Characters*, OH: F&W Publications, Inc.

Ocork, Shannon (1989). *How to Write Mysteries*, OH: F&W Publications, Inc.

Dincin Buchman, Dian & Groves, Seli (1987). *The Writer's Digest Guide To Manuscript Formats*, OH: F&W Publications, Inc.

Edelstein, Scott (1989). *Manuscript Submission*, OH: F&W Publications, Inc.

Holt, Robert Lawrence (1985). *How to Publish, Promote, and Sell Your Own Book*, NY St. Martin's Press.

Markel, Mark (1998). *Technical Communications*, MA: Bedford/St. Martin.

Scholastic (2000). *The Arrow Writer's Handbook,* NY: Scholastic.

Brusaw, Charles T., Alred, Gerald J., Oliu, Walter E. (1997). Handbook of Technical Writing, NY: St. Martin's Press.

Kramer, Jolie (1999). Story Structure for Novels and Screenplays.

Houghton Mifflin Company (1994). The American Heritage Dictionary, NY: Dell Publishing.

A Word from the Author

The most important words of advice that I can give to you are: ***DO NOT SIGN ANYTHING until you have it reviewed by a lawyer or an agent.*** Do not even make a verbal commitment. If you receive an offer from a publisher who wants to publish your book, simply thank them, tell them that you would like some time to consider their offer and ask if it would be all right if you got back to them in a few days. Then, if you do not have an agent or cannot afford a lawyer, do one of the following:

- Call some of the corporate law offices in your area and ask if they offer any pro bono services. If they do, explain your circumstance and ask if they have anyone who would be willing to take on your case.
- Do some research on the internet on agents, ask fellow authors for contacts and information on agents or invest in The Writer's Digest Guide to Literary Agents.
  (See http://www.writersdigest.com/store/booksdisplay.asp?id=10758 for more info.)
- After doing some research call an agent, tell them say that you have an offer from a publishing house and you are seeking agented representation.

Another book that you might consider investing in is *The Writer's Market*. You can find it at practically any bookstore or even at the library. It gives you an index to the publishing houses and editors that are publishing what you like to write.

Rejection is part of the business. Don't let it throw you. Don't let it stop you from getting to where you need to go. Remember that it's all up to you. You can let rejection stop you, or you can let rejection be the learning tool that it is. Rejection is just a learning tool for your eventual success.

If you do not own a computer, see what you can do about purchasing one.
If you don''t know how to use a computer, take some classes.

If you are going the traditional publishing house route, you must understand that publishers get a slew of manuscripts from all around the world. You have to make yourself stand out. You have to be unique and memorable. You have to make your work resonate. The way you do that is by first knowing your audience and then eliciting a strong emotional response in them. Another way to be memorable is to have a very unique and interesting premise.

If you are going the self-publishing route, remember that you can print as many, or as few books as you want. Your per-unit production cost drops dramatically with an increase in quantity. But the flip side of this is that the more you print, the more inventory you will be sitting on until it sells. And understand that even if you are self-publishing, there will people that you have to work with like booksellers, distributors, and wholesalers who will require a piece of the action in order to do business with you.

Be appreciative. When people do things for you, show your appreciation with a small gesture of some sort. Send them a free book or just a simple thank you card. Let your readers, publishers, agents, designers, editors... everyone who helps you to reach your goal, know that you appreciate them and/or their efforts.

Try as much as possible to treat people the way that you want to be treated. You will meet people from all walks of life in this business. Some of them will be nice to you and some of them won't. But the reality of the situation is that you don't know if that person who was rude to you is someone who could be a potential help to you in your career or not. And the flip side of that is that they don't know if you are someone who is about to blow up in the publishing world. So don't concern yourself with other people's negative energy. I say this because if you do blow up, everyone will remember you, including those who were unkind to you. And in that moment, they will remember what they did and so will you.

Like energy attracts like energy, so try as much as possible to stay on the a positive vibe. That said, my advice to you is to dream your dream. Go ahead. Dream your dream. Never lose sight of it, and never, ever give it up. Peace and Joy Until You Reach the Light!

Valerie Rose